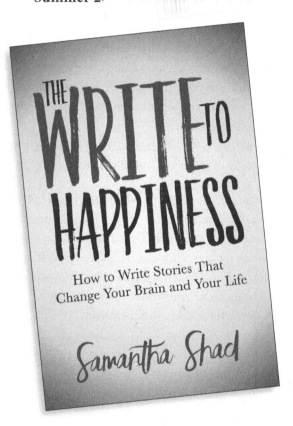

More on *The Write to Happiness*

Learn how your brain changes when you write…
why doing nothing at the right time can
supercharge your writing…why fictional
changes are real life changes…and more.

Rating: Excellent

"Veteran screenwriter Samantha Shad finds that stories are fertile ground for working out problems because narrative is the essential language of the brain. She packs a lot into her short, readable two-part book—showing first how to "write to happiness," and then giving the scientific reasons why storytelling works for your brain. By pairing a step-by-step guide on how to write fictitious, therapeutic stories with a survey of neuroscience and storytelling conventions, Shad shows with great empathy that making up stories is how humans compose and understand their lives. The brain is geared for stories, so writing one—yes, now you can—is a powerful way to understand and resolve life's dilemmas."

—getabstract.com

"Readers, prepare yourselves for an adventure. You are facing a master storyteller who challenges the reader with a book on reading and writing fiction. Things get even more exciting when Samantha Shad dives headfirst in brain sciences that participate in the creative process. This should be a warning for the reader to buckle their seatbelt for what Joseph Campbell once called the hero's journey. Ms. Shad is a storyteller (or mythmaker) on a hero's quest through a jungle of dangerous facts and poisonous footnotes. Follow her path and you will definitely enjoy, and perhaps profit immensely by following her on a journey into creativity and imagination."

—Jarrett Barnhill, MD, DFAPA, FAACAP, Professor and
Director, University of North Carolina Developmental
Neuropharmacology Clinic

"Samantha Shad shows us how each character in our story reflects a little part of ourselves and gives us the opportunity to sort out multiple approaches to *our* lives as we inspire the lives of our readers. As Shad writes, "Stories are problem-solving machines for the audience." If you want the rules for writing to happiness this is the book for you. Not only does Shad show you how to do it, she also explains what's happening in your brain as you engage your story, create your characters, follow them on their journey and, at the same time, have fun in the process."

—Maureen Murdock, author of *Unreliable Truth: On Memoir and Memory* and *The Heroine's Journey*

"This treasure of a book is a delight-to-read tool that shows how we can use our innate talent to tell stories to reprogram our lives. First prescribing the elements of a good story and showing how we can find them in our own lives, Ms. Shad then points to the latest scientific studies to authenticate her methodology. If you have a problem in your life that you can't seem to solve, this is the book for you."

—JoAnne O'Brien-Levin, PhD, Coaching to Wisdom Developmental Editor

"An intelligent, thoughtful, and thoroughly entertaining presentation of the best strategies and tactics for crafting the best stories. Samantha Shad is a master storyteller who now shows she is a master teacher as well. She knows how to unpack the powerful magic of story to help us all improve our use of story. I will refer to it time and again in my own work."

—Carl Nordgren, author of *Becoming a Creative Genius (again)*

"This brilliant book takes Story from its source in human development, through its connections to neuroscience. It is the most comprehensive melding of current thoughts on brain plasticity and Story's ability to affect our lives. I'd recommend *The Write to Happiness* to anyone who is serious about being a writer as well as to anyone who is serious about becoming a happier person."

—Beth Sullivan, creator and executive producer of
Dr. Quinn, Medicine Woman

"Wish I'd read this book forty years ago.... I could've spent a lot more time on the Riviera!"

—Arnold Shulman, screenwriter, *A Chorus Line,*
And the Band Played On

"What a truly useful guide to someone who wants to write a book. 'Take my hand,' says Samantha Shad, 'and let me show you how.' Then, she not only explains how to write your book, she also uses examples and explanations to demonstrate how writing your book can improve your life at the same time. Amazing! Wish I had this book years ago. Read it cover to cover and am keeping it for future reference. Thanks so much for the opportunity."

—Chrissy Jackson, Director Emeritus, Florida Writers Association

Write THROUGH THE CRISIS

MAKE GOOD USE OF BAD TIMES

Samantha Shad

AUTHOR OF *THE WRITE TO HAPPINESS*

Axillar Books

Write Through the Crisis

Published by Axillar Books and Samantha Shad
www.samanthashad.com

© 2020 Samantha Shad and Axillar Books

ISBN: 978-1-7338652-1-0

Send requests to publish work from this book to:
hello@SamanthaShad.com

———————

All of the profits from this book are donated to the Ronald McDonald House Charities of North Carolina.

Contents

"You never want a serious crisis to go to waste. And what I mean by that is an opportunity to do things that you think you could not do before."

—RAHM EMANUEL[1]

Stuck in a crisis?
This book provides a way
to turn problems into solutions.

Opening Notes

I'm a veteran of living through disasters.

Then I found writing.

It changed my whole life. And it can change yours.

My life was a catastrophe. I wasn't broke or quarantined, but I lived in constant crisis. I was deeply damaged by my mother, who was a psychopath. Her mother, in turn, had committed infanticide, so just surviving was a victory. I also suffered from the sadly common list of modern maladies: rape, abuse, and abandonment. Yup, one big fat crisis.

One day I sat down at a keyboard and started writing. Then I wrote more. And more. And then I became a writer, because the writing itself was a magic elixir for my soul. Each major piece I wrote helped me to heal and grow. After writing for a long time, I realized that I was happy, and writing had been the road to that better place.

I spent a lot of time researching whether there was any sound scientific evidence for my belief that writing saved me. I found a veritable mountain of scientific evidence for it, and I put that research into my book, *The Write to Happiness*.

Then came the pandemic. I had friends and students suddenly wondering what they could do at home. The answer was obvious to me: use it to write your way to a sweeter life, as I had done. You don't have to like living in disaster-mode, but you can use it to make your life better. I did. This book tells you how to make the best out of a crisis by using it to write yourself to a richer soul.

If the crisis hits you, then you're looking down the barrel of "social isolation" in a pandemic or a financial wipeout, family disaster, worldwide flood. You'll be stuck at home with too much time and not enough good company. You are about to be bored to death, as if ordered into an 18th century "confinement" for childbirth, updated only by an unlimited supply of repetitive Netflix originals. You can binge for a while . . . but only a while. Then the rolling carpet of what-am-I-going-to-do-today rolls out endlessly before you.

You need something. Something to keep your interest. Something to challenge you. Maybe something, dare we say it, productive?

That's right, never let a good crisis go to waste. Use it for yourself, for your growth, for your internal adventures, for finding new talents and old wisdom.

Yeah, you're ready.

You're ready to make lemonade.

You're ready to power through.

You're ready to produce the newer, better you.

You're ready to Write Through The Crisis.

Let's go.

Why We're Writing

Writing works.

It soothes the soul. It heals. It teaches, enriches, broadens, engulfs, challenges, and creates joy, meaning, optimism, efficacy, and connection with others.

When we write we fictionalize problems that are bothering us. We think we are just writing make believe, which is perfect. Our characters will face some problems that come from us, and then we, the distant writer who is pretty loose about the whole thing because, hey, it's just make believe, will find some solutions. And rework them so we can get to the end of the story. We finish a fictional story that has a make believe solution that our brain records as a real solution, untying the knot of trouble we started with. The fictional resolution literally changes our mind. That's why writing is so deeply productive to us.

Writing is engaging and soul enriching. Your confinement is a good time to invest in your enrichment. Writing is how you do it.

Start Here

The Baby Steps

You're not a writer, you say.

Maybe, maybe not, I say.

Want to find out?

We will start by just writing.

Get out a pen and a pad, and set a clock for twenty minutes. Yes, it has to be a pen or pencil, not your laptop. There are many times when a keyboard is equal to or superior to the slow, painful process of hand writing. This is not one of them.

Once you start writing, you have to keep the pen moving along the page without stopping. No thinking, no considering, absolutely no re-considering. The pen must keep moving, without even a hesitation, for twenty minutes.

Because you have no idea what to write, begin right now by writing the following sentence over and over until something changes:

I don't know what to write I don't know what to write I don't know what to write. . . .

Twenty minutes.

Go.

Checking In

After writing for twenty minutes, something happened. You hated it or you loved it or you wound up writing a love story about your cat and the cat next door.

It doesn't matter what you wrote. It mattered that you wrote.

Remember in Phys. Ed. that you always had to start class with warm up exercises, which, somehow, never in fact warmed you up? These are different. These are warm up exercises to loosen up the words that are already in your head. If you give them a way to come out, more will form. More will start looking for a way to go from your brain or your heart to your page. You want to open the sluice. Let the words come.

Write Again

Pen to the page. Write for twenty minutes, without stopping. Go.

Checking In Again

Writing begets writing.

If you aren't naturally a writer, it feels awkward. Repeat this exercise of writing whatever happens to flow out of the point of the pen for twenty minutes every day for as long as it takes. The rest of your life would be a good amount of time.

Two things will occur.

First, the more often you do it, the more easily words will tumble out of your pen. Good words, bad words, silly words, many words. You will find an ease with words. That ease will feed your future healing and growth. That ease pays enormous dividends.

The more you write, the more the writing talks back to you.

The more facile you become with throwing words down on a page, the more talented you will become in choosing words for their impact. You are becoming a writer by throwing words down on a page.

You are learning the craft of letting things stuck in your brain flow out of you.

Second, some change will come to the content of the writing.

Words will take on an order that is all your own. Or a subject that piques your interest will suddenly grow like a flower in the garden, on its own, with you simply watching in amazement. Words will suddenly alight to express an emotion. Or a dream. Or a story.

No one, not one single person of reasonably normal intelligence, can write "I don't know what to write" for twenty minutes a day, four days in a row. Sooner or later some emotion stored in your brain will overtake your hand muscles and something else will spurt out. It could be anger or love or fear of a description of a glass of water. When that small shift happens, follow where it takes you. If it's emotional, express it all. If it's a huge flurry of words describing the fly on your desk, get to it. If it's how your mamma was a sinner, spell it out.

We want to get comfortable with our words.

After that, we want to get comfortable with our thoughts.

This act is best accomplished by letting your hand do the writing and keeping your conscious mind out of the way. You are well acquainted with how to control thoughts, but less so at encouraging their free reign. Free flow is a good state to know.

Writing Everyone Can Do

Write a Journal

Congratulations, you are already doing this one.

Journaling is the beautiful stepchild of the diary. The diary is, in turn, the legitimate child of record keeping. Begun ages ago, our accountant forebears took copious notes of the commercial transactions that engaged them over distances. The practice of keeping a written record enlarged as people, self-importance in tight control, started keeping records of themselves and the things they did. Eventually, the diary of the day's events from the perspective of the diarist became popular.

The results were the full panoply of human spirits, the careful and the wildly uncontrolled, the selfless and the narcissistic, the historic and the insignificant.

The point of the diary was to record events, which in turn resulted in specific accounts of the quotidian. But the restless soul of writing, which encourages contemplation and reflection, could not be quelled. Keeping a diary became journaling.

The rules of journaling are wonderfully simple. Take out pen. Write for twenty minutes or so. Try to do it at the same time every day. Try to let the words flow freely, without editing.

Then step back for a moment, and consider what you wrote. Is there something to learn in those words? Something to observe? Either way, task complete.

Journaling has many benefits. It encourages the free flow of words, emotions, and thoughts from the brain, including our lovely sub-conscious, straight to the page. That, in turn, encourages reflection, reconsideration, and growth. Journaling grants us privacy with our inner selves. It elevates our self-reflection. It gets us writing.

Journaling regularly creates a sacred space, in your mind and your day, for yourself. Most importantly, if you journal every day, you are writing a meaningful piece to someone who is worth all that the time and effort: you.

Gratitude Journals

These take many forms, but it comes down to this: Write down 10 things a day that you are grateful for. Do it every day. The more you do it, the more likely when something good comes by, you'll notice it and add it to your bank of good things, and each time, you'll reinforce the positive habit of seeing the bright side. The results of gratitude journals are positive.

I was always highly suspect of gratitude journals. The practice seemed superficial and subject to unearned cheerleading.

Yet gratitude journals have some real benefits.

It makes you concentrate on positive aspects of your life. The more you focus on the positive, the more positive you bring in. Yeah, sounds like a bad lyric, but there's some truth lurking below. You are training your positive mind muscle. The more you exercise it, the more prominent it becomes in your physical brain. Your positivity network builds and builds, until, if you keep at it, you tend to default to the positive, which is a spectacular result. You have created the "have lemons, make lemonade" muscle in your brain and your mind.

Also, the act of taking a moment for gratitude disrupts rational processes long enough, even for just a moment, to derail a negative cycle. Again, the more you do it, the more natural derailing negativity becomes. If there's a place for an automatic pilot button in my brain, I want this one.

Gratitude journaling works for a lot of people. It's a great starter kit. For others, the journaling becomes homework, and the joy of feeling grateful gets linked to the misery of having yet another chore to do every day—and a boring one at that.

When it gets too boring or rote, plug in the lemonade maker. You are so good at it, it's time to move on to bigger, more elegant writing.

Back to the Future

What would happen if you thought about a future in which everything went right in your life? Sit down and journal for a few days about what your perfect future would look like. Then journal on what you did to get to that perfect place. If you contemplate the actions you took to get to your best future self, you will set out, loosely speaking, a series of steps that will take you to where you want to go—and have the additional benefit of avoiding having to dredge up all the things in your past that you just don't want to deal with. This practice encourages you to change your behavior first, with the hope that you establish a fortuitous beneficial cycle. It works.

Sit Down and Write to You

In 1935, Fred E. Ahlert (music) and Joe Young (lyrics) wrote a little ditty called, "I'm Gonna Sit Right Down and Write Myself a Letter." I know this little factoid because when I was a kid and hanging out in my father's office, a guy named Freddie Ahlert Jr. would often be there schmoozing away. Freddie's claim to fame was that he collected the royalties from his father's song. The song was recorded by everyone in a particular generation, among them Fats Waller, Frank Sinatra, Dean Martin, Ella Fitzgerald and . . . wait for it . . . Paul McCartney. I knew it by heart at the age of four and remember it as very '30s, lots of piano rolls, no guitar. Because of this peculiar personal connection, it remained categorized in my brain under "Freddie's little ditties."

It was pretty shocking to look at the lyrics decades later and realize I had to move them from "little ditties" to the "wisdom" category.

What would happen if, as the song suggests, you wrote some kind letters to yourself, ladling out affection and joy for yourself? There are no known studies on the effects of the Freddie Ahlert Song Test in modern social science, but I found it intuitively attractive.

When I was 15 and completely miserable, I would sit right down and write myself a letter. I addressed it to 15-year-old me, from a future happy me 20 years hence. I would explain the things that my future self was enjoying, the great things I had done recently, and my plans for my even more distant future happiness. I signed the letters, sealed each one in an envelope, and put it in a drawer for future perusal and reassurance. When the drawer was closed, I felt that everything was going to come out alright and, indeed, would think about how I would get from the miserable here to the happy there. It was a form of enforced optimism.

Many decades later, a heavy downpour wiped out the back of the garage that held my stash of keepsakes. I pulled out my most treasured shoe box and opened it. Inside the box were the last few pictures of my first true love and those letters written to my miserable 15-year-old self from a happier place in my fictionalized future. Everything in the box had turned into black liquefied gunk. Like a Pennebaker subject, I was momentarily saddened. I even got maudlin. I was in the rose garden of my Hollywood bungalow-style house in Southern California, the thick scent of orange blossoms picked up by the Santa Ana winds, the temperature that California perfect 72 or so. My only obligation that day was to love my daughter and maybe, just maybe, spend some time alone in front of the computer fantasizing about the imaginary people in my inchoate next script. I wondered what I had thought my life would be like in the letters. There I was, standing in the sweet sunshine, in that future I had dreamt of, and I was happier than I had ever imagined. The letters had done a good job. My first true love was still nowhere to be found, and I definitely hadn't traded up from him. But I had written my letters to me and that was quite good enough.

Try writing to your present self from your happier future self. It worked for me. And it's fun. Where else can you be the All Powerful One of your own life and feel guilt-free?

If you write it down, you are more likely to take the necessary actions to achieve the best possible you. These exercises put more than a smile on our faces. They help us change perspective and thus change our interpretation of events so that we take action that will more positively affect us.

Expressive Writing

Expressive writing is the name for an approach to using writing for its emotional benefits that was begun by James Pennebaker at the University of Texas in the late 1980s.

Pennebaker was interested in how writing, loosely in the form of journaling, impacted the health of his subjects. He had worked with the FBI on lie detector tests, and noted that they could be used to pressure those subjects to confess to their wrongdoing. The counterintuitive result was that suspects who confessed and thus elected to serve substantial penal sentences nevertheless felt better after they had unburdened themselves by admitting to their crimes.

Pennebaker wanted to find out if, more generally, confessing one's secrets had the same positive effect. In his very first study, he gathered fewer than 50 students and asked them to write for 15 minutes a day for four days.[2] By a flip of the coin, the students chose whether their assignment would be to write about a traumatic topic or a superficial, non-emotional topic. A typical expressive writing exercise asks the subject to write for 15 or 20 minutes continually, four days in a row.

EXERCISE: DAY 1

➤ Please write about an event in your past which you remember as traumatic or upsetting.

➤ Please write without stopping. Do not be concerned about spelling or grammar.

➤ Write from your deepest emotions, knowing no one will see this writing except you.

Try it. Yes, you reading this. Give this exercise a go.

If you tried this exercise, you've gotten through your first bit of expressive writing. If you are by nature a writer, the words probably flowed easily. If writing is not naturally your thing, this exercise is another way to loosen up that muscle. Now take the post-writing survey:

POST-WRITING SURVEY

Please complete the following:

0	1	2	3	4	5	6	7	8	9	10
Not at All				Somewhat				A Great Deal		

1. To what degree did you express your deepest thoughts and feelings? _____

2. To what degree do you currently feel sad or upset?

   _____

3. To what degree do you currently feel happy?

   _____

4. To what degree was today's writing valuable and meaningful for you? _____

5. On separate piece of paper, briefly describe how your writing went. You do not have to share the content of your writing. Rather, write about your experience of writing about your traumatic experience and your feelings about it then and now. Reflect on your experience of writing your story.

On the second day, do the following exercise:

EXERCISE: DAY 2

➤ Today, please write about an event in your past which you remember as traumatic or upsetting.

➤ Please write without stopping. Do not be concerned about spelling or grammar.

➤ Write from your deepest emotions, knowing no one will see this writing except you.

Yes, Exercise 2 is the same as Exercise 1. Did anything new come up for you?

Follow each day's exercise with the post-writing survey.

EXERCISE: DAY 3

➤ Now shift your writing so that you are considering the topic from a different perspective or different point of view.

➢ Write about how this event shaped your life and who you are.

➢ Explore, especially those deep issues about which you may be particularly vulnerable.

EXERCISE: DAY 4

➢ Now stand back and think about the events, issues, thoughts, and feelings that you have disclosed.

➢ Really be honest with yourself about this upheaval and do your best to wrap up your writing about this topic in a meaningful story that you can take with you into the future.

Pennebaker's initial studies randomly divided his subjects into expressive and control groups. Twenty minutes, four days in a row. How important could 80 minutes be?

Expressive Writing Results

Well, pretty important.

Pennebaker wanted to quantify the health effects of expressive writing. He measured those effects by how many illness-related medical visits the subjects had before and after the experiment. In the six months after the first study, the "expressive" writers had *half* the number of visits to the health center compared with the control group. Immediately after writing, the subjects experienced increases in feelings of anxiety and sadness, but they also expressed a greater sense of meaning.

Pennebaker repeated the experiment four times before he published his results.[3] The expressive writers cut their visits to doctors by 43% over both the non-expressive writers and non-writers three months after the experiment. If fewer doctor visits means you are healthier, then these results were a smashing success.[4]

What about the anxiety or sadness after the writing exercises? Intuitively, you can sense that writing about a troubling experience would bum you out. But months later, the subjects overwhelmingly described the process positively and expressed the impact in terms of gaining insight into their lives. The results were not an expression of momentary relief of stress, but rather something larger and deeper: insight.

Social scientists need money for research, and they need measurable results to demonstrate the potential benefits of their studies in order to keep those research funds flowing. Pennebaker's results turned on the spigots of research and hundreds of studies of expressive writing ensued. All those experiments produced voluminous information on the health effects that were the initial focus of all the studies.

Early analysis of how writing affects the body showed that the immune system is enhanced. Chronic illnesses like asthma and rheumatoid arthritis show improvement. AIDS patients show increased white blood cell counts. Cancer patients show a reduction in symptoms, a reduction in overall pain, better sleep, and higher daytime functioning. Relatively healthy adults see a decrease in blood pressure and lower liver enzyme levels. Arthritis and lupus sufferers report decreased fatigue. Physiological indicators of stress also show a decrease. Writing about past failures appears to decrease the stress we feel when we face a stressor in the future.[5]

One explanation for these results is that the writing may allow the writer to adapt both cognitively and behaviorally to a new, immediate stressor. Pennebaker was looking at stress levels at the beginning of his work. He found out, ironically, that writing about what stresses you actually de-stresses you.

Now, after almost 30 years of study, the list of benefits of expressive writing is so long that it makes you want to just go out and buy a bottle and chug that expressive writing right down. Here's a partial list:

- Fewer stress-related visits to the doctor

- Improved immune system functioning

- Reduced blood pressure

- Fewer days in hospital

- Improved mood/aspect

- Feeling of greater psychological well-being

- Reduced depressive symptoms before examinations

- Fewer post-traumatic intrusions and avoidance

- Improved social and behavioral outcomes

- Reduced absenteeism from work

- Quicker re-employment after job loss

- Improved working memory

- Improved athletic performance

- Higher student grade point average

- Altered social and linguistic behavior

Am I saying that a measly 80 minutes can change your life forever? I am completely dubious. If an hour and 20 minutes could change lives, wouldn't the entire population put in the time so we wouldn't have to talk about finding happiness because we would already have it? I had been trying to change my life for decades, the thought that a quick fix could work made me feel, well, stupid. And yet . . .

One study followed 100 middle-aged engineers who were fired from long-term jobs with a company that was downsizing. Most of the men (yes, all men) had been with the company for many years, and all of them were at that certain stage in life when employment opportunities dry up. All the men were still unemployed six months after they were laid off.

At the six-month mark, the men were divided into an expressive writing group ("writers") and a control group composed of men who either did no writing or wrote about the emotionally flat concept of time management ("control group"). The writers were asked to write their deepest thoughts and feelings about getting fired. The men wrote for 30 minutes for five days in a row. Three months later, 27% of the writers group had landed jobs, but only 5% of the control group. Seven months later, 53% of the writers group had jobs, but only 18% of the control group.[6] For a majority of the writing group, the two and a half hours they spent writing changed their lives profoundly.

Two and a half hours!

You could do that tonight and watch a movie.
It works!

Understanding Your Own Writing Results

If you aren't a middle-aged unemployed engineer, is there a way to look at your writing and gauge your own experience? Early on, researchers found that the more optimistic the writing, the more likely the exercise will have positive effects for the writer. Knowing this, try another expressive writing exercise:

You've already written for several days.

Today, look at the events you wrote about and try to see them from another perspective.

➤ Is there anything you missed that you want to cover today?

➤ Loose ends?

➤ Perhaps a different perspective or point in time?

Write for 15 minutes, four days in a row.

What Your Writing Can Tell You

Take a look at your writing, literally, as though it were a picture.

What does your handwriting look like on the first day? Is it loose or tight? Big or small? Careful or explosive? Compare the first day with the last.

It's common for people to become more comfortable both with the exercise and the content of the event they are writing about, so the handwriting becomes looser. Did that happen to you? If it got tighter, did it happen as you went deeper into recalling an event? Did you correct your writing as you went? Did you cross out words, make corrections, or use good grammar? The more corrections, the more it indicates that the subject is concerned with the writing, as opposed to the content of the event.[7]

How was the *content* of the writing? Because this whole field was begun by social psychologists, there are algorithms for everything. How many happy words? How many sad words? And in what ratio? How about the number of pronouns? How many "thinking" words? Can we predict who will benefit from expressive writing before we go off wasting two hours of our life in the search for profound change? Consider these results:

The more *positive emotions* you include, the better. Positive words, like "love" and "joy" are indicators of an optimistic attitude, which is a fine thing to have all by itself. It also allows the writer to acknowledge positive emotions even when dealing with traumatic events and suggests a capacity for coping with setbacks.

Negative emotions? You're writing about things that bother you, so by definition, you are going to be negative. Try some moderation on for size. See if it sticks. People who use a lot of negative words like "afraid" or "hate" don't enjoy great benefits from expressive writing. People who use a moderate amount and acknowledge the feelings do well with expressive writing. It's as if putting it on the page and acknowledging it allows you to move on in your life.

Lots of *pronouns*. Really, pronouns? Yes. Lots of "I" and "me" at the beginning of the writing? Fine. Increasing the number of pronouns as you progress, lots of "you," "they," "she," and "he"? Great. That shift to more and different pronouns comes about when you change perspective. If you start out knowing it is all about you but end up viewing it through other people, that change in perspective gives you distance and context for viewing the experience. It breaks you out of a narcissistic or childish view of the event and forces you to be objective or more adult. It takes the sting out.

Stories help us. Now, I truly believe that the power of storytelling is the greatest power known to humankind, and I'll make my case for that later. For right now, let's acknowledge that the algorithm people agree on is that as you move toward building a story about a painful event, you do a few productive things. First, stories play out with a kind of universal structure and series of cause-and-effect moments. Building a story in this way means you are considering what caused the trauma and searching for ways to escape from the same situation in the future. Constructing a story builds hope. It builds a sense of efficacy because, as we work within the framework of story, we build our tools for overcoming obstacles.

If we use what are called "insight words" like "realize," "know," and "understand," we are indicating a stepping-back from immersion into the event and toward a third-person or objective point of view. Taken together, using story markers, insight words, and cause-and-effect words like "because," "reason," and "effect" show the greatest improvement after expressive writing. The more your writing pulls you toward story, the better writing will be to you in return.[8]

How did knowing which elements indicate positive results affect your writing? If you know that positive words or pronouns or any of the elements directly help you in gaining positive results, does that change anything? When I have taught this material, I tell students that the more positive their writing, the more likely they will have good results. The students then write more positively and have better results. Is this a good thing, or is it cheating on the test?

The answer is yes to both choices. Knowing that positive word choices give "better" results is a priming experience, leading us along the road we would want to go down anyway. It may be cheating, because you know what works, but it also helps you learn how to make it work.

Theories and Explanations

Pennebaker had initially theorized that expressive writing worked because inhibiting uncomfortable memories causes stress. Releasing those inhibitions would free up a lot of that energy and allow us to focus on more conscious and pleasant experiences. Confession releases the inhibitions, and catharsis results. Everyone feels all better. Eureka!

This preliminary explanation, called *disinhibition*, was elegant and simple. Suppressing memories causes stress on the body. Release the information, and emotions come pouring out of you. The stress-inducing thoughts appear on paper instead of in your brain, the inhibition is released, and the world is good.

For people who had never spoken of a hidden, dark secret, the theory can work. It's useful for those who have been repressed.

Getting it off your chest is good.

For some people.

For some of the time.

For a while.

It works.

Kinda.

Another explanatory theory for why writing works is that it causes a *cognitive change*, which is the social science way of saying we look at our experiences differently. As we get more comfortable with the writing and the experiences it expresses, we may change the voice we use (changing to third-person point of view) and alter the overall tone (using more positive words).

When we repeat the exercises, we tend to put the events into a narrative form. From a subjective or random order, we tend to put the events into a chronological, and therefore more rational, order. Eventually the events may be presented in a cause-and-effect manner. Each of these changes brings us more consciously and objectively into seeing the experience in a more rational and less emotional way. That takes a lot of the sting out of bad memories—letting the past come into conscious awareness without all the stress.

So then, is expressive writing the silver bullet and now you can close this book, spend 20 minutes a day, four days in a row and completely transform your life?

If only.

The more research that was done, the less clear the results were.

First, the paradigm was developed, not in the real world but by social scientists working on campuses. We are talking academics in search of research money and tenured chairs.

As a group, they are particularly defensive about being "social," not "real," scientists. They seek research money by proving that they have "results" and "measurables" and "data you can replicate." These are not the men and women of metaphor or transformational journeys. These are the measurers. They design experiments that can be populated with always-available college students, usually healthy, young, and of short attention span, who are willing to participate for a few hours for a few bucks or a few credits. The birthplace of this paradigm meant the results would be quantitative and limited—not deep, wide, or transformational. We can judge their results with their own tools: small, replicable, and often shallow.

Even with that proviso, the results of all that research were mixed. Yes, many people saw positive results. But while people high in the ability to write expressively about emotions had less anxiety three months after the end of a study, people who were not good at expressing emotional issues in writing showed a *significant increase* in anxiety. Expressive writing was *detrimental* to childhood abuse survivors and Vietnam War veterans with PTSD. Writing is ineffective when dealing with normal grief. People who just blew off steam in their writing without making other changes had negative results. The outcomes were mixed for victims of natural disasters and broken relationships. Pennebaker himself has concluded that "as you will see, writing doesn't work for everyone. The effects are typically modest but usually beneficial."[9] Like other social scientists, Pennebaker and his progeny's pursuit of the measurables leaves them without the deep, long immersion that fiction writers experience.

Is expressive writing just a baby step? Sophie Nicholls,

the head of the Humanities Department at Teesside University and a novelist, sees expressive writing as a rung on a larger ladder of developmental writing. Nicholls knows what it means to spend more than a grand total of 80 minutes, but rather months and maybe years focused on writing a single complex story.

For Nichols, "In developmental creative writing, the writer gains some initial release from writing her feelings out onto the page and then moves on to begin to shape her material, learning to craft and redraft it, ultimately developing a new relationship with aspects of her self-experience, perhaps by experimentation with form, perhaps by fictionalizing or retelling the initially expressed material from a different point of view. . . . Significant insights and understandings are gained as the writer works through further phases, gradually becoming a "reader" of herself on the page and developing a greater reflexivity of self-understanding."[10]

I agree. Expressive writing can be just the appetizer for the delicious seven-course meal your writing can serve you.

Why Does Expressive Writing Work?

So why does expressive writing work? I think that it helps non-natural writers to construct a story, and as any natural writer knows, constructing a story makes you make sense of the material. The closer Pennebaker's subjects came to writing a story or a narrative, the more positive were the results.

If you write out what happened to you, you are likely to move toward putting events in a chronological order. And if you have a chronological order, some events will become cause and some will become effect. Things will begin to have a reason for happening.

Maybe other participants in the event will make their presence known, thus changing the perspective of the writer. Adding another person's view gives us distance on the event, which has a defusing quality. Over time, as we develop a narrative, we have a comprehensible explanation and, because our brains have limited real estate, we can take the explanation, tuck it away in a nice, efficient place in our memory, and *stop ruminating about it*. Because it makes sense, it takes up a lot less room in our heads and frees us (and in particular, our brain's working memory) to either think other thoughts or, best of all, have some free space to just be present in the moment.

In the end, expressive writing can produce some miracles and many a smaller change, but the meta-analysis is decidedly mixed. The Pennebaker branch of the writing tree can confuse writing and typing. There are benefits to be gained by sitting down and putting a lot of words on a page, but it isn't qualitatively the same as throwing down a garbage draft and then working the structure to create a well-developed story.

What can we conclude about expressive writing? It caused a seismic change in how academics and mental health practitioners looked at writing. While previously viewed as the often somber purview of baroque romantics, writing for the self was reframed as a health-inducing, soul-enriching, stress-reducing practice. The simple joy of sitting and writing, enjoyed by many an artist and introvert, got the stamp of approval as self-help of the very best kind.

Expressive writing is health writing. The more you do

it, the more likely you will experience meaningful growth and joy.

Expressive writing is also a gateway drug. The more experience one has with it, the closer we are to the writing that transforms lives.

Every expressive writing exercise brings the author one step closer to the miracle of writing stories. Indeed, fictional stories are not just a joy to compose, but the change agent that transforms lives.

The Power of Story

Write a Story

The language of story-telling is often invoked when we go on significant personal journeys, and for good reason.

We are to be strong protagonists on our own journey. The parallel between the language of story and the language of self-development is a rich vein to pursue. I suspect it is often used as a Tony Robbins–type pep talk, "Be the Protagonist in Your Life! Start Today!" The depth of the parallel is belittled by the clichés.

Narratives put events in an order for us. If you begin writing with a chaotic view, once there are a few events in a sequence, the order of the scenes develops an organizing principle. Perhaps the events are chronological. If you write a story told in the first person, the order may not be the chronological order of events, but rather the order in which they are discovered by your protagonist. Action and reaction follow each other. A change in perspective is comparable to *reframing* a situation, and we can look at it not as the irrational event that made us feel powerless and victimized, but rather as a rational, empowered individual in an objective, rational situation. When we include other characters' points of view, we necessarily change our subjective perspective.

Someone else's perspective can change you deeply. If you or your main character is busy whining about some injustice and another character says, "Hey, you are just whining. Grow up," then in the process of writing the next line of dialogue, you will have to answer that charge. How does your character respond? "I'm not whining!!!!" tells us the character is too defensive. What gives? Or if the character says, "I sound like my mother," well, that's a very different way for the character to view herself. No matter what the response your character gives, you've been engaged to question what's really going on with your character, and you'll have to answer that question to continue in the scene.

When we write a story, we take a series of events and explain them in a way we think someone else could understand them. As we explain these events to someone else, we explain them to ourselves. Conversely, we can't explain to someone else if we don't understand it ourselves. Writing a story makes us explain it to ourselves.

Go write a story.

Follow the rules of good storytelling: a first act that explains the world as it is; a second act filled with plans, obstacles, and setbacks; and a third act that requires a new integration of knowledge and a resolution. Make sure your protagonist learns something, so you can learn it, too.

Write a good story.

Checking In

Did you write a story? Any kind of story? One sentence? A paragraph which ended in mid-sentence? Forty pages ready for Knopf?

All good. In fact, all equally good.

It doesn't matter where you start. It matters that you tried to write a story and you have something in front of you that is a beginning.

It matters because real stories, ones with some basic format and structure, are different from anything else you will ever write.

Real stories are tales of more or less courageous people facing problems and learning skills on the way to victory or defeat. Along the way, you will choose to believe it is all make believe, and that security will make you, the writer of the story, brave beyond all imagining in the pursuit of solutions to worthy problems, and your character will learn, grow, and enrich her soul.

And so will you.

Let's write a great story.

Why Writing Stories Works

Writing fictional stories is the exercise of our imagination in creating worlds of our making, with characters that are parts of us, facing problems which perplex us, to a resolution that enriches us. Oh, wait. That's for the professional writers. Let me try again.

Writing fictional stories is the exercise of our non-professional imagination in creating our own worlds with characters who are parts of us, facing problems we amateurs are perplexed by, to a resolution that enriches us.

Okay, same thing.

Regardless of one's level of expertise in writing, the application of a few of the simple rules of storytelling that have survived millennia will lead us to writing stories that also heal us. Forget about the lofty title "writer" or the importance of sentence structure and word choice. The benefits flow from writing your own story, in your own words, provided only that it a real story and not just a catalog of things that kinda happen, with no direction. You can write a fictional story. You can. Really. Don't aim for literature. Don't aim to replace John Grisham. Just write a story that only you will read, following the few rules of storytelling. It will change your life. It transformed mine.

What Happens in Your Brain When You Write a Story

If you want to just jump to writing stories, please do so.

If you wonder whether the happy talk—that you can change your life by writing stories—leaves you skeptical and you want a more substantial explanation, buckle up. Here it is.

Consider this writing process. We will call ourselves writers. We are not passive couch potatoes. We are creators. We choose the emotions, actions, and words of each of the characters. We are *actively* in the consciousness of all the characters involved. And we feel empathy and understanding for each and all of them. We choose each behavior of each person in the scene. To accomplish this amazing trick, we go into the mind of each of the characters and *simulate* all the possibilities for emotions and actions that we can think of for each of the characters. We aren't just simulating a perspective. We are a multidimensional interpersonal simulation super-consciousness. We have felt and thought through every possibility we could imagine, multiplied by the number of characters in the situation.

So let's review. You and I, the writers, let our sub-conscious come up with an idea about something that is bothering us. We write a story, following the basic rules. We experience the problem from every perspective we can think up. We try every solution we can imagine, for every character. We writers have had to experience the internal world of the bad guy or antagonist in the moment of victimizing us, the protagonist. Our view of the antagonist must change. When that happens, our view of the protagonist—that is, some version of ourselves—also changes. When our hero realizes this new synthesis, we realize it, too. As the character is changed and victorious, so are we. We now have the all the knowledge gained from inside each person's head as they behaved in interaction with each other. We've absorbed the growth of the protagonist, the empathy of the fearsome but defeated antagonist, the synthesis by the observer, and the integration of the reader.

Our brain broadly speaking has two large networks that are relevant to our tasks. One part is rational and conscious. It is what happens when we are concentrating on a task. The other part is called the Default Mode Network (DMN), and it is what turns on when our rational brain turns off because we are "doing nothing." We are staring at the ceiling or daydreaming or picking weeds from the garden. We feel like we are doing nothing, but the Default Mode Network is actually the center for processing our selves, our relationships with others, and other social connections. It is where we daydream. When we are doing rational tasks, the Default Mode Network turns off, the rational network turns on. When we are "doing nothing" the rational network turns off and the default mode turns on.

But not when we are writing. What happens when we turn our focus to working on a story or trying to figure out what our main character is going to say to the antagonist in the next confrontation? New research indicates that there are a few types of tasks relating to the self and social interactions that engage *both* the default mode and other, conscious operations of the brain. The DMN is activated ("on") during conscious tasks like episodic and working memory, forecasting, emotional processing, and, most importantly, the interpretation of narratives.[11] In other words, during the process of creating narratives, we use the DMN *plus* other networks. Creative writing is different than almost all our other activities because it adds more areas of the brain to the activity. More of our brain is engaged. More brain with fewer filters means more neuronal engagement, which in turn creates more connectivity, which causes more neuroplasticity, which means we have more learning, which means we have more change. Again, your brain is on fire in a way that is more intense and unique compared to all the other ways you use your brain.

That's why you can write to happiness. Because writing is that much more intense, active, and involving. While you are writing fiction, you are not just "like" the character before you, you *are* character. You ponder the choices, make the decisions, play out the scenarios, and gain or suffer the consequences. This is so much more than merely simulating some possibilities. This is *living the possibilities*, and the choices, the changes in perspective, the wisdom, the failures, and the rewards—all in the first person. When we write fiction, we get so fully engaged that we are said to be transported. With transportation theory, which is a genuine scientific analysis of what happens, we _are_ the character. What that character learns, we learn. Our brains change to include the new knowledge, the new wisdom, the new perspective. We write our way to a better us.

Good storytelling is not easy. It requires finding real solutions to our fictitious obstacles. Good storytelling requires that you find a genuine resolution and write a real ending. And when you do, you—in the real world—have encoded those lessons and perspectives into your own mind, through the combined miracles of transportation, mirror neurons, simulations, and the great exercise of neuroplasticity. You have focused and reworked and paid so much attention to your writing that the highways of your brain have been rerouted and you are, indeed, the hero of the journey. You have managed to do this remarkable work from the comfort of your own desk, in your jammies, without breaking a sweat because it was always just fiction, you were never really physically at risk, and your interpreter sewed it all up. You believed it was real, so the _changes in your brain are real._ You emerge no longer an innocent with obstacles, but an adult who has resolved the problem of the past and integrated the information you may always have had into a new wisdom. You can throw off the old baggage that slowed you down. You've written yourself to greater skill, understanding, and happiness.

Find Your Own Story

The Writer

Great stories aren't written by plumbers or statisticians. Great stories are written by writers.

A writer is a person who is comfortable putting words down on a page and who is willing to look back at it to make it better if necessary.

You've already accomplished these tasks in the earlier exercises. You are already a writer.

In fact, you have done so much great work that you can switch from pen to keyboard as your chosen instrument. That's right, you can speed write for now on, if you want to.

What else is involved in being a writer?

It requires a bit of thought.

It requires something more than typing.

It is more organized, and more beautiful, than hurling a bunch of words across the room aimed at your screen. If you do that, you'll have something, but it's not a story. It's an impulse or an inspiration or a word salad or, worst of all, a list of facts. It will suck as a story.

How do we write a story? Like cooking a meal, we'll start with a list of the ingredients. We'll find the nub, the story, the characters, and the obstacles. When we've assembled them in reasonable proportions, we'll process them so that it becomes more of a story and less of a pile of words.

Writers come in two favorite flavors.

Plotters sit down and figure out every twist and turn in a long outline before they write a word of prose. Later, they will struggle to bring vitality and life to the story.

Pantsers sit down and write by the seat of their pants without an organized plan and stop writing when they get to the end. Later, they will struggle to bring focus to their stories.

Which flavor of writer are you?

It doesn't matter.

We are all both types of writers, at different times. Pantsers are better at finding and following creative ideas. Plotters are good at cleaning up a creative mess and making it comprehensible to the audience. It isn't a straight line. We alternate without all that much logic.

If you find you suddenly want to veer off because you've had a great thought or a transfixing idea, that's great. That's your pantser-self having a moment. Follow it. But you have to come back to the place you were before your idea pulled you to the juicy piece of story that was waiting for you.

We'll lay out the way to write a great story here as if it is logical. We'll pick out the essential elements of a great story and build on them in sequence.

Break out of this orderly approach any time your inner pantser has her moment. Then you must come back to add the elements of a great story.

We start by finding the *nub* of the story, which is the arena in which the story takes place.

We choose a temporary main character and a goal that expresses what we're thinking about.

Then we figure out what stands in the way of our main character achieving the goal.

After that, we can define our characters.

When we have the nub and the main character, there will be certain challenges that the hero simply must face. We'll make a list of those challenges, and that will be the outline of the whole story.

It looks simple and orderly. It is neither.

The Imaginary Audience

The difference between a story and all other writing forms is that story structure was developed to keep an audience interested in the information presented. From earliest times, when the "storyteller" was a guy in front of the tribe miming out how to use a spear so the group could get some fish and not starve to death, to the great storytellers of today and tomorrow, how the audience, whether real or imagined, would react to the story is a crucial element. Story structure and its elements developed to maintain interest, and also to add important information under the guise of entertainment. This system works brilliantly and stories are universally enjoyed through the world, and throughout time. We *Homo sapiens* developed with exquisitely designed brains that take the meaning out of stories and store it for later use and growth.

When we write for our own enjoyment or growth, we follow the rules for engaging our imaginary audience because our thousands of years of evolution have taught us that our growth and survival are both increased by implementing those rules.

The rules of storytelling deliver important lessons in growth and enrichment in a structure that has been refined over the millennia to fulfill that purpose. If you want your writing to enrich you, you have to follow those rules. So imagine you have an audience, even an audience of just one person, for whom you are writing. You never have to show your story to anyone, but you do have to write it as if you will.

The Nub

"I want to write a story about _____."

The blank is the nub of your story. The sentence might be "I want to write a story about . . ." death row, snowboarding, pumpkin festivals, sex in space, Tomorrowland.

The nub of a story is something that is bothering you, the writer. It is the arena in which your actual story will take place. Perhaps it's something you've read online or you've been dreaming about. Squibs of thoughts and printed articles pinned on your wall are nubs of a story. A lot of writers have a file tucked away of little tidbits that are so unformed that you can't even call them ideas. Those are nubs. "I want to write a story" that's about family dysfunction. In a hospital where everyone gets sick(er). About that guy on death row. Each of those is a nub. It's not yet a story or an idea or even much of a thought. It's an area or zone you want to explore.

Can you fill in the blank?

I want to write a story about _____.

If you can do it in five words or less, you have a nub, and you're ready to expand it to an idea.

The Idea

Every story starts with an *idea*. How do you find your idea? When do you know you have it? This is the formula an idea:

A CHARACTER has a GOAL, but there is an OBSTACLE.

When we can fill in the blanks in this sentence, we have an idea. Can you fill in these blanks?

_____ wants _____ , but _____ .

The usual order for finding your idea is to find the nub of it, put in a placeholder for the hero, determine the goal, and figure out what is standing in the way.

How to Find Your Story

Here is the most important thing in the whole wide universe about finding your story: **It doesn't matter how you find your story.**

Seriously. Great stories drop from the sky or sneak into your sleep or slap you in the face. It doesn't matter where they come from. It matters that they visit you and you are brilliant enough to pay attention.

Writing a story that can change your life means allowing material that is bubbling in your non-conscious mind to come to consciousness in some form that isn't too frightening. The beauty of this truth is that no matter what you are writing, the material will float into your consciousness and your writing as long as you let it.

We've been trained to control our sub-conscious and dampen down the crazy ideas it throws into our consciousness. Not now. As writers, we honor those thoughts because we know our best material floats around in that boiling cauldron of crazy to marinate. Give your subconscious a hug. It's part of you, and there's plenty of good stuff down there. Maybe if you give it a little respect, it will send you some great ideas. Love your subconscious.

In terms of your writing, your non-conscious mind holds voluminous material. When a non-conscious idea bubbles up, through a dream or in meditation or daydreaming, respect it. Understand that you are receiving your best material. Your non-conscious mind is your friend, and it will send you what you need. When your idea veers off in a strange direction, follow it. The key, again, lies in not getting in the way of the idea that is ready to tap you on the shoulder.

So how do you find your next story? There are two ways:

1. Go out and search for it.

2. Sit back and tell it to find you.

Both approaches work. I personally prefer to tell it to find me, because while I'm waiting, I can get a lot of gardening done.

1. Go out and search for it.

Searching for an idea means researching until something captivates your interest. Swim in the news media. Read web pages, blogs, newspapers, news feeds, gossip sites. Read all kinds of stuff, and pay great attention to what nags at you. If it nags for more than ten minutes, print it and tape it to the wall. It must be physically in front of you, somewhere you might see it when you aren't looking for it. You can't get this done by putting it in electronic form.

You're just cleaning off your desk and you keep checking out this one sheet you have about the guy on death row? Great. The fluff piece about a Silicon Valley exec who you just know can't be as good as his press? Good. Your sub-conscious will turn your attention to a page or two hung your wall. As always, trust your sub-conscious.

If you have a few nubs, go online and research them for real. You will bring focus to your search. Research tells the universe that you mean it and that it should show up to help you.

The point of flowing in the river of information is to see what piques your interest. Even though it may look quite goal-oriented, this search will give you a sense of freedom.

Remember, you are looking for an idea, not the perfect idea. There are plenty of good ideas out there. Grab one. If you wait for the perfect one to hit you, you will never get started. As the master himself, Steven King cautions, "Let's get one thing clear right now, shall we? There is no Idea Dump, no Story Central, no Island of the Buried Bestsellers; good story ideas seem to come quite literally from nowhere, sailing at you right out of the empty sky: two previously unrelated ideas come together and make something new under the sun. Your job isn't to find these ideas but to recognize them when they show up."[12]

Looking for a commercially perfect story idea is like sending out engraved invitations to the judges, editors, superegos, and all the forces of your internal universe that can say "no"—and inviting them to party in your brain. This approach manufactures procrastination and frustration. We are looking for the story that will help you write to your richer self, and worrying about external success won't get you there. Neither will stories intended to please others instead of yourself.

2. Sit back and tell your idea to come find you:

My favorite way to find an idea is to do nothing. Stare at the ceiling. Go for a run. Take a long, aimless drive. Walk with music blasting through your head.

Keeping your mind relatively empty of ideas and external focus will free up your brain to float around and make associations and connections you wouldn't otherwise entertain. In turn, this allows those pesky little issues that you keep repressed in your sub-conscious to swim about in your most creative brain space. Doing nothing is very fruitful for creative production, and there's a ton of science to back up the great benefit of doing nothing.

Techniques For Opening The Door

The purpose of your concentration on doing nothing is to let your non-conscious mind come through with ideas so you can catch them before your conscious mind slaps them back down. The right idea for you will be something that you don't want to face head on. You open the door to that idea by giving your conscious brain the day off.

There are a lot of ways to accomplish doing nothing.

Dreams are a glorious source for your idea. When you are going to sleep, make the conscious decision to dream for an idea. Do it for several nights in a row. When you get up, make notes about your dreams. Ask yourself what the dream felt like and which problem it seemed to be looking at. After a few days, lay the dreams out in some order and look for the common elements in them. What's popped up several times? Whatever it is, there's your story idea.

Journaling is a form of actively doing nothing. You've already tried it, so now that you are looking for a real story, give it another go.

Meditation works, although it throws some curve balls at creative types. If you are comfortable meditating without further explanation, then pursue it. Most of the creative people I know can't meditate worth a damn. They try to clear their heads of ideas, but the things just insist on shooting into their minds. Or it clears for just the shortest wisp of a second and then, wham! That itch of a thought comes flying in. Those writers spend their energy chasing ideas away.

Here's the good news for writers: Forget about the directive to rid your mind of your thoughts. If you are a writer and, while meditating, an idea comes in that just won't go away, *follow it.* If ideas are coming to you while you meditate, open the door. Follow where the lightning bolts lead you. Line them up, see what the common nub is, and write it down. Your idea is in there, trying to come out.

There are a few other methods that can allow your bubbling idea to come out when you aren't looking. Doodling while you are doing something else (usually a boring conference call) can lead to useful thoughts. Painting works. Long showers work. So does taking a long drive. So does riding a bike. Think that's nuts? That's what Albert Einstein was doing when he came up with the Special Theory of Relativity.

All of these activities work because they keep you occupied. This frees your non-conscious mind. Material you would ordinarily smack down can now bubble up and reach the surface. It makes space for ideas that you wouldn't consciously choose to work with. *The material that has to sneak up on you because you really don't want to deal with it right now is exactly the material you need to deal with right now.*

Let it come up in fictionalized form. It's easier on everyone that way.

Finding Your Idea: A Hypothetical

Here's an example of how I look for an idea:

My conscious thoughts had been revolving around the information in this book. But I just couldn't think of a fictional idea to use as my example of a story in this book. I wanted it to be useful to you, the reader, interesting enough so that you didn't throw the book across the room or shut it down—and universal or impersonal enough so that you wouldn't know too much about me.

It was a difficult series of needles to thread, with a typical series of requirements: Don't be boring; don't show the writer's personal wounds; don't, don't, don't. Then for two of three nights, I had dreams about a credit I gave up on for a film that later surprised everyone with accolades. Why hadn't I fought for that credit? It either got lost in my divorce or wasn't worth the fight, but now, decades later, my sleepy-smart brain was still irked. Of course, the dream also included space ships, Angola State Prison in Louisiana, and my usual lost cellphone, but the center was that crazy old credit I never got. Two nights later, there was a dream about my father's old record collection. When he was a kid, he bought two copies of each of the great jazz performances of his day. He played one of each, but saved a pristine copy of each of these performances, unplayed and in its original sleeve. In the dream, I couldn't get to them, couldn't find them, and maybe even didn't search for them very hard. They were taken by someone. The taking was a betrayal.

In real life, I hadn't thought about that record collection for a long time, and it had been literally five decades since anyone had played or paid attention to the collection. I can't say that the record collection mattered in any concrete way. I didn't know if the records had any value, though I had always expected to donate the unplayed 78s to my alma mater's music school. Someone would want them, I thought; someone might listen.

These two dreams were about the same thing: In the dreams, someone took something from me that I felt was deservedly mine. That is the core of what is bothering me now, in my life. My dreams were telling me what my conscious mind would never allow to come to thought: that I felt betrayed and that it really bothered me. That's what the story has to be about, because that's what's trying to break through at my vulnerable time, when I am asleep: stories of betrayals and loss.

In this arena, I wonder what kind of loss—right now, a loss of a thing, a record collection and a credit. What do they have in common? Well, they are physical manifestations of creative work. Hmm. . . . That could be the theme, but that's running ahead of myself. Right now, I know only one thing: to write about a betrayal, a loss of something valuable and ephemeral.

That's a nub.

Your Temporary Main Character

Your temporary main character is a distant version of you or an unrepresentative slice of you. Bigger or smarter or stupider or younger or whatever. A different person who happens to have shared a partial Vulcan mind meld with you. Give the character a name that sounds completely different from your own.

Choosing a name that doesn't sound at all like your own helps create distance between yourself and the character. Give the main character the freedom of having a distinctive name and the interesting peculiarities that will come with that. You won't be particularly self-conscious or protective of a character that has a very different name from your own.

For this one moment, a temporary name for the protagonist is perfectly fine. We'll come back to the main character later, when we need her input on the story.

I usually use Maxine, Grace, or JoAnne for my temporary character names, because I don't know a soul with those names. Grace sounds soft, even graceful. Gracie is even better. I'll use that. Because we will follow the development of this story and because the main character is female, let's refer to our hero as "she." It's appropriate for our hypothetical story, and the world could well use more female heroes.

How much of a story idea do we have? Let's fill in the blanks.

Gracie wants an ephemeral item.

Okay, it's a beginning. Let's put some story meat on those bones.

The Goal

If you have a main character operating within an arena, you are ready for the next step. Ask your character what she wants.

Every good story has a character who wants something. Having a goal is essential. At the beginnings of the story, the goal is often general. In a lawyer story, the lawyer usually wants to win the big case or make partner. In a medical story, the doctor wants to cure a disease. In both of these arenas, the goal may be to find success, whether it is making partner or getting a key position in a prestigious institution or a remunerative specialty. In the movie *Black Panther*, the new ruler wants to be a good king. In *Mandela*, Nelson Mandela wants to establish racial justice.

The goal has to be specific and succinctly stated. If you need to explain the goal, it's not ready. If it takes a paragraph to describe it, it's not ready. If your main character is a writer, she must want something we can hold on to: perhaps winning a Pulitzer. Or writing a bestseller. Or she has a condition or disability, and the writing is only a collateral issue. Choose one, but only one goal.

New writers regularly rebel against finding a specific, simple, singular goal. They believe they have a more interesting and nuanced view of the character and therefore they must present the many external and internal meanings of the goal. It is absolutely true that the writer must have a nuanced understanding of the character and her relationship to the goal. You will use that knowledge to describe actions and present dialogue that resonates and has subtext. However, if the goal is "nuanced" at the beginning, the likelihood is that the reader will have trouble understanding it as first presented, and the story will be muddled. Additionally, you the writer will not be able to distinguish between what truly matters to the story and what is mere surplusage, which you convince yourself is "depth."

If you start with a complicated or unfocused goal, you lose your reader and your direction. If you start with a simple goal, but you the writer understand that there is more to it than at first appears, you grant your audience the gift of discovery and growth as the story continues.

Defining the goal may require a bit of psychological excavation. I had a student who had a story about a young doctor who wanted to be a dermatologist. The writer was absolutely certain about that specialty. It took a long time until she could go deep enough to realize that the character wanted to be a dermatologist because it was an easy specialty that made a lot of money and thus she would have a cushy life with a big house.

It's important to know *why* your character wants that particular goal. In the medical story, dermatology was code for, "I want to look like a specialist, but I don't care much for curing people; it's all about me the doctor." In defining the goal of the character, these material aspects were crucial not only to the character, but to everything that followed. If the core of the character was essentially a physician who didn't want to work hard, everything about the story will be different from the medical story about the doctor who wants to cure cancer because her mother died from it, or the poor kid who got into medical school because the income is good and his family needs money.

Here's the fill-in-the-blank for your character:

My character wants or wants to be a(n) _____ because/for _____.

In our hypothetical, what's Gracie's goal? Here's a way to work it out: What was taken from her? I take out a piece of paper and list a bunch of things that could be stolen from her:

- an heirloom
- a byline
- a diamond
- a necklace
- a piece of gold
- a record collection
- a car

Whew, those are all over the place. But what interested me at the beginning was the odd value in my dreams, the ephemeral value of a screen credit, the historical but not financial value of a record collection. Somehow, it's not about overt, objective value. In the dreams, the value was emotional or interpretative. I don't want to use the record collection in the story: It's too personal to me, and I will feel too vulnerable to dig deep into the emotions I would feel if I use it. I need something like the record collection or creative credit—but more comprehensible to the audience.

- A fictional McGuffin, like an award given to an ancestor would work.

- Grampa's Oscar?

- Mom's wedding dress?

- How about paintings?

Mom's wedding dress is very sentimental. Grampa's Oscar tells the audience that it's a story about the movie business, but that's not what I want to write. But a painting? That could work. Some art that hung in the character's home and which she always expected to inherit. Yes, the art might have an objective value, but it has the emotional pull; it was in Dad's study when the character was growing up. Dad even promised it to her. Okay, the thing is a painting that had been promised to her. I imagine the painting as pretty big and well-framed but not on a hook. It's leaning against the wall, propped up on a table with books holding it in place.

Gracie wants the leaning painting.

All we need now it to find *the BUT*.

The But

In all good stories, we have a protagonist who wants something but is stymied by the BUT, the thing that stands in the way of the character and achievement of the goal. Within the idea, there must be conflict. If it's just a thought—"I want to be a doctor"—there is no story. There is a subject, medical studies, but nothing happening within it. A story always has a BUT. "I want to be a doctor, BUT I don't have the money for med school."

Here are a few examples of the BUT:

"I want to save my brother BUT he's on the other side of the war zone." (*1917*)

"I want to experience the dinosaurs, BUT they could turn on me." (*Jurassic Park*)

Mandela wants to lead a revolution, BUT he's in jail for 27 years. (*Mandela*)

Every love story: "I'm in love with somebody, BUT that somebody is far away, married, from the other side, dead, or otherwise unavailable."

"I want to be a best-selling writer, BUT I can't hold a pencil." (*My Left Foot*)

"I want to be a successful lawyer, BUT I just screwed up the only case I have." (*The Verdict*)

"I want to change the world, BUT I'm being sued by the moneybags for stealing the idea." (*The Social Network*)

Your idea is the arena or question you want to look at. The BUT makes it into a storyline. Once the BUT is added, it's a story because you have added a direction to the narrative.

For example, if Mandela wants to lead a revolution but he's in jail, how can he accomplish his goal from solitary confinement? The BUT leads to a series of questions your story must answer. How can he communicate to the outside world? What does he want to communicate? If he can't go outside, that is, effectively lead the free people of his country, can he go inside, that is, inside himself for a different vision?

If "I want to be a doctor" is the idea, then what is stopping your character from becoming a doctor? If it's because the character doesn't have the money, a world has opened up. The question you will pursue is this: How do I find the money to become a doctor?

The <u>BUT is the thing that stops your main character</u>. The BUT is the reason your idea isn't just a topic, but an issue with direction and energy.

The BUT is the obstacle that will define your hero's journey. Can you fill in these blanks with very few words?

My character _____ wants _____ BUT _____.

In our hypothetical, what is the main character's BUT? Why can't Gracie get the painting? Make a list of reasons Gracie can't get the painting:

- It's been destroyed by a fire? By an act of vandalism?

- It's still in the study, but the lock has been changed? By whom? Can she get a key? Does her demented mother have it? Another member of the family for safekeeping? Another member of the family as a theft?

- Has it been stolen? By a robber? By friendly fire, that is, someone Gracie knows?

- By someone with legal rights of some sort? A creditor? An executor of the will?

- By the will because her father gave it to his mistress? To his illegitimate son, the brother Gracie never knew she had?

It's been stolen. I like it.

Okay then, how did the painting get stolen? Did someone sneak into her father's home and steal it? Maybe. Maybe the house was lost in foreclosure. Or the painting was sold at the estate sale when the house was liquidated. Or the executor of the estate sold it off. Any of these will do. If it was sold at the estate sale, then we have a story of tracking down the painting from a possibly innocent party. What obstacle poses the greatest challenge to Gracie? A thief makes the story a mystery. The demented mother makes it a family drama, which is likely to deal with the problems of the mother and other family members, not Gracie's sense of being betrayed. In a fire? What does that do to Gracie's goal?

Does she give up? Does she fight for insurance money? Are either of those satisfying? I like the executor-of-the-will idea. It's a soft theft, not an at-gunpoint event, but a dramatic conflict. It opens up a lot of juicy questions: Who is the executor? In whose interest is the executor acting? Another family member's? His or her own? Some faceless, impersonal authority that can't recognize the emotional value of the painting? Yup, I like the executor idea; it gives a lot of juicy possibilities. The executor won't give Gracie the painting.

If the executor sold it, then we aren't going to be that interested in the painting, but we are going to want to know what is going on with the executor. Did he or she lie to Dad about the estate? Did the executor take advantage of Mom, who is suffering from dementia? I like the executor line better because it gives the story a real antagonist. It gives the story more emotion: conniving in the past, betrayal of trust, what kind of person steals from an estate they are serving? That's it. Here's our story idea:

Gracie wants the painting that hung in Dad's study, but it was stolen by the executor.

Break the Glass Solutions

If you've tried everything but are still devoid of an idea, rejoice!

Your brain doesn't care whether your story ideas are true or not, real or not, or even original or not. Your brain just wants some story to work with. If you're ready to break the glass, do what the professionals have done since time immemorial: Lift someone the great body of old stories. Lift from

Shakespeare or the Bible or The Grimm Brothers. We all get inspired by what has come before us.

If you have any dream of publishing—and you should carry that dream—then please lift only from public domain sources. With that very small caveat, lift away.

If you are truly hugging your unconscious, fear not, for it will send you the material you need to look at this moment in your life. It won't be what the Grimm boys or the bard had on their minds. It will be original with you, and you will bring that originality to the page. Stories that have lasted throughout time present a smorgasbord of good material that will help with the selection and cultivation of internal themes.

Try a fairy tale. Check Google and Wikipedia and make a long list of all the elements of a fairy tale in all its various versions. At a recent seminar which only allowed for 20 minutes for finding the idea, I asked students who had no current project to look at my list of story elements from "Little Red Riding Hood" to pick out the five elements they liked the most, and to build a quick story on those, and only those, elements. Here are the elements I found in some of the many versions of "Little Red Riding Hood":

Little girl

Walks through creepy place

Has orders from her mother not to get sidetracked

Carrying goodies for older relative

Mean wolf

He wants her and the food

Girl naively tells him where she is going

He diverts her by telling her, "Go get some flowers."

Wolf goes to relative's house

Gains entry

He locks relative in closet

He kills relative

Girl arrives

Grandma looks strange

Relative says, "What a deep voice, the better to greet you with," cat and mouse game

Wolf destroys/consumes girl

Wolf sleeps

Guy with tool arrives for other reasons

Guy with tool uses tool to destroy wolf, free girl

Girl and relative are rescued and are unharmed

They fill wolf's body with rocks/concrete

Wolf tries to escape

Wolf collapses

Relative hides in closet

Girl escapes with help of guy with tool before being consumed by wolf

Wolf forces girl to take off her clothes

Clothes thrown in fire

Girl escapes into the woods

Wolf ties a string on her

Girl does or doesn't slip the string off

Wolf chases after her

Girl escapes with help of another woman, e.g., laundress who puts taut sheet over river, girl climbs over it

Wolf follows and is consumed by the river

Girl listens to wolf's advice on the road, thinking him wise

Girl passes through woods filled with lumberjacks

Wolf consumes her; the end

Stranger with tool is a lumberjack she passed along the way

Lumberjack is a stalker

Stranger with tool is a huntsman wanting the wolf's skin

Relative and girl set physical traps for wolves for their skins

Girl is in love with unsuitable guy, a lumberjack

Girl is betrothed to attractive (rich) suitor

Girl's sister is betrothed to rich suitor

Girl's sister is murdered

Girl's sister is murdered by fiancé

Girl's sister is murdered by wolf

. . . and a priest comes to town

IT TAKES PLACE:

In the 9th century

14th century

17th century

20th century

21st century

THE BEAST IS A:

Wolf

Tiger

Ogre

Werewolf

RELATIVE'S BODY IS:

Unharmed inside the beast

Left in parts (and girl eats the meat, cannibalizing grandma)

THE RELATIVE IS:

Grandma

Mom, unbeknownst to Girl

Girl's evil sister who deserves to die

Each student picked five elements and strung them into a single sentence. One student told the tale of rape in a Western town in the 1840s. Another told the story of a bitter feud between a mother and daughter during World War II. A third wrote a steamy forbidden love story about Red and a Baptist preacher in the South during the civil rights movement.

Each of us will choose the elements of the story that speak not just to us, but to the part of us that is simmering just below our consciousness. The woman who wrote about rape in a Western town was struggling with sexual abuse. Expressing the real trauma in her life was too difficult for her. But writing a story about someone who was definitely not her, just an imaginary person in a place and time she had never visited, gave her enough room to allow the emotions and problems of a sexual abuse trauma to rise to the surface. This was her story idea, and the longer she followed it, within the strict confines of a fictional character in a specific time and place, the easier it was for her to access the very real emotional issues that the rape elicited and to present a riveting and timely narrative.

However, Little Red Riding Hood was developed at a time when women were victims and heroes came in late in the story to save them. You can make Red the hero anyway, and that's an empowering story, or you can choose a different fairy tale.

Hansel and Gretel is a similarly rich fairy tale. Here are some elements to the tale:

THE CHARACTERS ARE:

A boy and a girl

Two boys

Three children

One child, one bird, one leopard

Father

Wife

Girlfriend

Grandmother

Ogre

Space alien

AT THE BEGINNING:

THERE IS A SHORTAGE OF:

Bread

Money

Animals for hunting

THE PARENTS TRY TO:

Sell them

Send them into woods to die

Send them away

Father agrees with plan to leave them to die

Father disagrees and fights it

Father disagrees but is too weak and relents

HANSEL AND GRETEL OVERHEAR:

Stepmother planning

Father planning

Story of the local church selling children

HANSEL:

Locks them into their room

Sneaks out and gathers sparkling stones

Does nothing

THEY ARE TAKEN INTO THE WOODS:

For the first time?

For the only time?

THEY BRING:

Nothing

Sparkling stones

Their cat

Sawdust

THEY ARE LEFT IN THE FOREST AND:

No one comes

A woodsman comes and kidnaps them

Robbers come and steal the bread/sparkling stones

THEY FIND THEIR WAY BACK WITH:

Stones

Breadcrumbs

A worn path

THEY ARE LOCKED IN ROOM AND:

Children sneak out and get stones

They get a piece of bread

They get their cat

They gather useless flowers

They are left in the forest and try to get home

Try to get home but the bread crumbs are gone

A river has washed away the house

They are kidnapped by cannibals

THEY FIND REFUGE IN:

A gingerbread house

A church

A village

THE PERSON WHO FINDS THEM IS:

A mean witch

A nice but blind grandmother

A priest

The evil woodsman

Magical animals that lead them to safety

THEN:

They are imprisoned in the barn

Sold to a childless couple

Sent to an orphanage in another country

Die of starvation

THEY STEAL:

The witch's jewelry

The church's bread

The woodsman's tools

Nothing

THEN:

They go on to live a life of plenty

They try to return to their home

The father is dead

The stepmother is dead

They hide on a boat going to America

They hide with a mission going to the Vatican

AND THEY:

Die

Use the witch's jewels to buy a happy home

Find their father and live happily ever after

Wind up on New York's Lower East Side where they open a bakery

IT TAKES PLACE IN:

13th century

700 B.C.

18th century

21st century

22nd century

WHERE IT TAKES PLACE:

Germany

Ireland

Africa

Mars

If you're stumped trying to find a story idea, choose a fairy tale. Pick five elements you like, change the time and location, and write your story. Write it as if it is your own, because it will become your own as you write.

If you're a pantser and you've been wanting to follow your ideas and write, write, write, then this is the time to do it. Go write for a while. Ask your characters who they are. What they are afraid of. What they want. What they hate. And what the heck they are doing. But remember, you have to come back.

Character

What is character?

Character has two relevant definitions. First, a character can be a role in a fictional piece, the *dramatic persona*. The father of the bride or the boss are dramatic roles. Such characters tend to have specific ages and particular physical features. Often, these are the people you wind up with when you use software or questionnaires to define your characters.

Second is the question of *character*: the ethical or moral standards at the heart of the matter, or the internal landscape that affects the external behavior. Simply, *the heart of the person*.

As writers, when we speak of character, we speak of this internal landscape brought out by behavior. While there may be many roles in any piece, this heart and soul is the character of your hero and also your villain. It always means the sum of the spirit and emotional history of the person and the behavior that we can see as a result. It is deeper and more significant than a role, and it is what you want your main character to have. If we want to touch the soul of our readers, we must share our own. Character is the map of the nooks and crannies of the heart.

For our purposes, "character" *always* means this internal map or psychological picture of the person. It is *never* the physical description of a person in your story, though if physical descriptors of any sort help guide you to their internal material, that's certainly useful.

Are your protagonist and antagonist always two people? What about a group or a team or a force? What about the ensemble piece?

Let us not get too literal about this question. We are writers and if any group of people in the world gets a little leeway on defining the rules of our craft, it's definitely us. Of course there is latitude in our presentation of our story. In *Star Wars*, The Empire is the antagonist . . . but it is an antagonist personified in individual characters. In *E.T.*, the scientific community that wants to study E.T. is the antagonist.

An ensemble piece can have quite a few main characters, but few of us have the skill to present a big group of main characters and still maintain the focus of the reader, so instead we have a character or two who stand out and encapsulate the qualities we are dramatizing. An effective ensemble piece requires, at minimum, a large body of information on each character, backstory, plot, and the like. With the possible exception of farce, the whole idea of an effective ensemble piece may be an oxymoron. It only works in a farce because the genre itself gives up on backstory and reason. Similarly, in a romantic comedy, there are theoretically two main characters, but surely there is one who is more broken, more romance averse, more blocked by the obstacle. The fact that two people are falling in love does not mean you have two heroes.

What about all the other roles in your story? Your protagonist and antagonist need to be well-developed and nuanced because the character of the protagonist and antagonist determines a lot of your story. The characters of the other roles don't serve the story, they serve the main characters. In other words, they can be important, but they are ancillary to the core of your story. When you have a story idea and maybe a few other scenes or elements of your finished product, you need only two roles: Your protagonist, the person we will root for, and the antagonist, the bad guy or person who stands in opposition to the protagonist. These two people will embody the conflicts, both internal and external, that form the core of your writing.

All the other characters, romantic interests, threshold guardians, comic relief, ghosts, mentors, the whole bagful of people you will need later on to tell your story are just distractions now. Put them back on the shelf. Tell them you'll get to them when you need them, and not a moment earlier than that. We can add the love interest and the mean boss later. Don't get sidetracked.

How to Develop Characters

Like so much of the creative process, it doesn't matter *how* you do it. It matters *what* you wind up with. Many writing teachers will tell students to fill out biographies for their characters: where they live, what schools they go to, what color hair they have. There are plenty of ways to generate characters, including software that will ask you what it believes are the important specific elements of a character. If software helps you find your character, great.

Any process that helps you discover the heart of your character is a good tool. However, please remember that all the externals—like the schools they attend and the color of their hair—can never be the heart of your characters. Those externals are the tools for navigating to the heart of the character, not the character itself. For example, let's say you have a character who went to Harvard. What does that tell us? Smart, probably, but not much else.

The follow-up questions might help. Why Harvard? Was she a legacy? That tells you something about how she was brought up and therefore could lead to her assumptions about her life. She went to Harvard but waited tables and ate spaghetti for four years to get by? That's a different character.

Wait, she went to City Junior College? Why did she go to a local junior college? If it's because her mother is ill and she has to be around to care for her, that's one character. If it's because she almost failed out of high school because she was dating the local bad boy who is in prison now and she can't get into any other school, then that's a very different character. In each of these examples, the exterior characteristics are useful only to the extent that they lead you to the character's heart.

Disregard people who think a character and a role are the same thing. Your reader, whether imaginary or real, is wiser. Your audience doesn't care about the externals, and there is a pile of science to explain why.

Main Characters

Your story needs a *protagonist* and an *antagonist*.

The protagonist is your lead character, the hero that the audience will follow on the journey that is your story. Your audience needs to root for the protagonist, so that character must be sympathetic, relatable, and active. Is there one word that encapsulates all these flying adjectives? Yup. Your main character must be *bondable.*

Your protagonist must be so relatable to your audience member that they will automatically, non-consciously identify with the protagonist. That does *not* mean the character has to be nice and sweet. It means the audience member can see a behavior and think, "Wow, I know what that feels like." This explains why a character with perfect taste and manners may not "get to us," but a character whom we meet when she is puking from being too drunk last night grabs our heart.

The antagonist is the person or force that stands in constant opposition to the protagonist. She is the bad guy, the evil one, the black hat.

These definitions appear simplistic and wooden. The characters will become more interesting and nuanced as you develop their internal lives and put them into active situations so their behavior expresses dilemmas within your story. In short, they are stiff right now.

They will develop into interesting characters because you will bring them to life. Be patient.

How to Develop Your Protagonist

Ask your main character to join you for tea. Really. Or for a chat. Or a walk. When looking for the outlines of the character, we want to know why this particular person wants that particular goal. In our painting hypothetical, does she want the painting because she thinks it's actually worth a bundle of money? Or does she miss her dead father and it reminds her of how much he loved her? Or did her mother always lust for that painting and if Gracie winds up with it, it's a "fuck you" to mom? Obviously, the possibilities are endless, but the choice you make is important. Each one of these choices tells you something different about Gracie's heart, and therefore much more about the journey she's beginning.

How do you find your character?

We want to have heart-to-heart talks with our characters, just as you would with a friend. We want to know what's the best thing that happened to her today. What's the worst? Does she have a big laugh? Does she have a bunch of pals or just one or two buddies? What do *they* talk about? What's bothering her today? What's just annoying? Is her house neat or a wreck or just a room she rents with some people she doesn't actually like? What's she afraid of today?

Idea maps are a great way to open the door and allow the character bubbles to get to the surface. It's free play, and that is absolutely the right way to approach it. Giant sheets of paper are a good start. So are colorful pens and markers and dancing music. Put your character's name smack in the middle of an oversized piece of paper and ask her what she loves. And what she hates. Why she wants goal. What it means to her. Keep going.

Once you get moving on an idea map, some of the spokes will have more energy. Follow that energy, because it's also your enthusiasm.

Another way to find your main character is to talk with her. At the keyboard, write the dialogue you want to have. And let your character answer. It might feel awkward for a few minutes, but if you can withhold judgment, characters often get chatty and will lead you right to the juice. If you have software or macros for writing scripts, use them. Call yourself the writer, and call your character by whatever name she's using.

                    WRITER
          Hey, Gracie. What are you up to?

                    GRACIE
          I'm hanging out waiting for you to ask
          a good question. You got one?

                    WRITER
          Wow. Hostile.

                    GRACIE
          ....!

What does the character say in response? Whatever it is, it tells you something. "Hey, sorry about coming on strong" reveals a different person from "I've just been waiting to get the painting, what's the holdup?" and "I'm not some friggin' rose on the vine, y'know!" Whatever the comeback is, you'll know your character a lot better. Keep at it.

If nothing else works, fill out the dreaded biography, remembering that where someone goes to school or lives or what they drive doesn't matter. Why they made those choices matters a lot.

The Perfect Fit

You now have your hero, an imperfect person with emotions. And you have a *problem*, which is the gnarled center of your idea. Why is this particular character the exactly perfect person to face this specific problem? When you can answer this question, you have the skeleton that will be your entire story. It's simple, but it ain't easy, as many a wise man has said.

Your protagonist will be someone who is broken in exactly the place where your story will challenge him or her. In a love story, the happy bachelor meets the perfect woman but is unable to commit. Why is he unable to commit? A broken heart from a first love? A mom who loved him so much she will never be equaled? Or a mom who loved him so little that he's become programmed to reject love?

In *Black Panther*, T'Challa wants to be a good king for his isolated country, but the outside world (in the person of Killmonger) wants to blow it open. What is the perfect fit for T'Challa? He adores his father and seeks to follow him, but his father's isolation for the country produced the evil that T'Challa now faces. His dedication to his father is in direct conflict with the needs of his people.

In *Spotlight*, the story of the journalists who broke the sexual abuse scandal in the Catholic Church, Robby, the hard-charging journalist, is determined to publicize all the Church's horrible offenses. What is Robby's wound that makes the fit perfect? Robby is a Catholic with a history of giving the Church a pass on its misdeeds. The closer Robby gets to the criminal priests, the closer he gets to the wound of his own subtle complicity. His wound, the complicity, is a perfect fit with a story line of righteous exposure of wrongdoing.

The perfect fit often pits the external goal of the character in direct conflict with a preexisting emotional or moral wound that is expressed in the *backstory* of your protagonist. Backstory, when used well, is not "what happened before the story begins." Backstory expresses your protagonist's preexisting emotional condition or the wounds which caused her to be hurtled into this specific story to begin with. Backstory is useful when it reveals what is in the character's heart.

As you write the full story, you will have to decide when to show the reader the backstory or wound. In *Black Panther*, T'Challa's particular wound is disclosed over the first two acts of the film. In *Chinatown*, Faye Dunaway's character finally tells us that "she's my sister *and* my daughter!" late in the film. In *Spotlight*, we discover in the very last scene that Robby had a dark history of giving the Church a pass on previous abuses. The choice of when to tell the reader why the obstacle and the character fit each other perfectly is determined by when you as the writer believe that the revelation will have the deepest resonance.

However, you, the writer, must know why your main character and the main obstacle form such a profound challenge before you travel into your story. You may not be telling your real or imaginary audience, but you will know it and write with that shadow, so that when it is fully revealed, the audience will feel the full depth of the dilemma. What you know about the character and what you tell the reader about the character are two separate things.

The Antagonist

Your *protagonist* needs opposition that personifies the reason why your hero hasn't already achieved her goal. The opposition can be a person, force, institution, even The Empire. This is a force or a person who opposes your hero and will do everything he/she/it can to prevent your hero from achieving the goal.

The *antagonist*, whether a person or a force of nature or whatever else, is what or who your hero is up against. Your antagonist deserves real time and development. He or she must have the resources and the will to be overwhelming. What tools does the antagonist have? Let's consider some examples:

In *1917*, the German army is the antagonist.

In *Mandela*, the antagonist is the South African government and the laws of apartheid.

In *E.T. the Extra-Terrestrial*, the antagonist is the whole humanoid world, including scientists and our so-called modern technology.

In *The Fugitive*, Gerard, the Tommy Lee Jones character, personifies the relentless determination of US law enforcement.

In *The Untouchables*, the antagonist is the mercilessly violent mob boss, Al Capone.

The smarter/better/more brilliant your antagonist, the better your hero will be forced to be. That is exactly what you want. So, to find your antagonist, the map is pretty straightforward. Given the obstacle you've chosen for your story, who is the one person you can conjure up who can impede the hero in the strongest way? Really? Make the villain stronger! Smarter! More powerful!

Who is the perfect villain in our painting hypothetical? The role of the executor already has a lot of power because in an estate situation, the law is on the executor's side. Who would be the most challenging executor for Gracie? We could consider the relationship the executor has to Gracie. Is he the trust department guy from the bank? A relative who is a lawyer, maybe Uncle Alan? How about a rich relative, like Cousin Jack? Each one gives the story different angles.

The trust guy from the bank would have a lot of authority and the bureaucracy of the bank and the courts on his side, but the role doesn't inherently bring much personal juice. Uncle Alan, the lawyer, will have specialized knowledge of the law, and, to me, a righteous attitude that will grate against Gracie's emotional reason for achieving her goal. What about a relative, a rich aunt or uncle, or a Brother/Cousin/Nephew Jack? A relative brings more raw emotions and attitudes. A brother makes it a sibling rivalry story, and that isn't quite right, I think. A cousin, though, a cousin could work. What could make a cousin more formidable? A guy, I think, because maybe Dad thought Gracie would benefit from a strong, male figure? How about a rich cousin, someone Dad thought would look after Gracie but who is full of himself and out to grab more than just the painting?

What if Dad thought that Cousin Jack would be perfect to help Gracie, so Dad gave him extraordinary powers expecting him to use them for Gracie's benefit, but Jack just wants to take over everything? He's got money and he's got apparent authority from Dad. That's a worthy opponent. I'd use him. Why does Gracie want the painting? Is it because it is valuable? Or because it represents her relationship with her father and she is jealous of sharing him, in whatever manifestation, with anyone? If that's why she wants the painting, then Jack is the perfect antagonist because he covets not just the painting, but its underlying emotional value, the connection with Dad. Jack's an antagonist with an emotional investment, the powers of the will as executor and the power of plenty of money. He's a great antagonist because he has all the power. Gracie has all the determination. This will be a good fight.

Conflict

"Conflict is the basis of drama."[13]

"Conflict must be at the very hub of your story, because it is the core of strong action and strong character."[14]

So sayeth the gods of screenwriting.

The job of the writer is to keep the reader interested right through to the very last page. Keeping it interesting is a way of keeping our focus on the things that are important. We keep it interesting by keeping our characters in conflicts.

What, then, is *conflict*? It isn't chasing someone around in a car, nor is it punching someone's lights out. It isn't yelling, running, or shooting.

Conflict occurs when two parties hold deeply held opposing positions at cross-purposes with each other. If one character believes in the right to an abortion and the second character believes life begins at conception in a story about football or cars or life on Mars, these characters aren't in conflict because their opposing positions aren't relevant to the story line. If the same two characters are in a domestic drama and one character is a pregnant teenager and the other is her mother, that's a conflict. Two people or two forces with inalterably opposing positions confronting each other is a conflict. That conflict drives the drama of your story.

In the film *E.T.*, E.T. just wants to go home. The adult scientists want to keep him here to study him. There is no middle ground. He's either on earth or not.

In the movie *The Untouchables*, Al Capone wants to have a liquor business. Elliot Ness wants to enforce Prohibition laws.

In the film *Mandela*, the protagonist wants equality for all people. The South African government wants apartheid.

Expert writers use direct, strong conflicts. Newbies pull their punches. Be forewarned: The less the drama, the less the interest. Don't commit the boring.

Your protagonist and antagonist must embody direct conflict in every story point.

Without direct and intense conflict, your story will fail. Make sure your protagonist and antagonist have a true, deep difference of positions.

The Obstacles

> *The basis of drama is . . . the struggle of the hero towards a specific goal at the end of which he realizes that what kept him from it was, in the lesser drama, civilization and, in the great drama, the discovery of something that he did not set out to discover but which can be seen retrospectively as inevitable.*

—DAVID MAMET[15]

What is preventing your hero from obtaining her goal?

The answer is the center line of your story. Your audience wants to see its hero face a series of ascending obstacles. What are the most challenging obstacles? Write them down.

Think you've come up with enough challenges? Write down more and more and more.

As Kurt Vonnegut advises, "Be a sadist. No matter how sweet and innocent your leading characters, make awful things happen to them, in order that the reader may see what they are made of."[16]

Write down at least 10 things that can go horribly wrong in your story, and make sure to include the worst things that could happen. Be a sadist.

What can the all-powerful antagonist do to harm our protagonist, slow her down, impede her path? Write down at least 10 more things that he can do to harm her, block her, and steal her goal again and again.

What happens when she loses everything?

Be merciless.

Plotting

We know what the protagonist and antagonist want, and we know some of the particular strengths they each bring to the conflict. So, what's the plot?

The plot is the ordering of the obstacles our protagonist must face on her journey to attaining her goal. Now is the time to consider the long list of all the obstacles that could possibly stand between her and her goal. Are the tests she will face severe enough?

Take out your list of obstacles.

Don't worry. This is the fun part.

We want to present our protagonist with the deepest, most juicy challenges along her road. Pick out the five to ten absolutely harshest obstacles for your protagonist. These are your character's *terribles*. Now put these in order, the least terrible of the terribles to the absolutely worst terrible. This is the *spine* of your story, the second act.

Each obstacle is increasingly difficult for your protagonist. By the end of the second act, everything has gone wrong. Every possible terrible thing has happened.

And then, indeed, *all is lost*.

The most common thing new writers get wrong is failing to put the protagonist through hell. They take it easy on her. They pull punches. We all fail in this way because we care about our characters and frankly want to protect them from our own worst instincts. But when we are protective of our protagonist, we cheat our audience members of any satisfaction because they want to learn from our protagonist. They, too, want to experience the joy of finding new strengths and wisdom. When you go easy on your protagonist, you deny your audience the opportunity to grow and learn . . . and you deny it to yourself.

The end of the second act must present a challenge to which you don't know the answer.

We writers avoid our deepest challenges in real life because we doubt we can overcome them. But our protagonist is fictional, unblocked, free of our own traumas. This is the very point where you must trust your protagonist beyond the extent to which you trust yourself. Trust her. She's fictional and free from all the other baggage. Trust her to take a leap or see a piece of wisdom or find a special tool that her creator, you, didn't know she had.

This is the very moment of transformation. All you need to do is to trust that your character will figure it out, though you may spend a few days stomping around waiting.

Better Obstacles

Do you have a fantastic list of obstacles to frustrate and test your main character to her core?

Probably not. More likely, you have a list of obstacles that you think are pretty tough but can be overcome. Ornery but doable. We need more. Make a list of the most heartbreaking setbacks you can imagine for your hero. Betrayal? Yes. Abandonment? Yes. Death of a beloved? Yes. Complete and absolute failure? Yes. Her own death? Yes.

Your list of obstacles must be the things that are *the most difficult* you can imagine for *your specific protagonist*. If right now, as you are writing, you can imagine a way out of the problem, then it isn't a big enough problem. What is it that—when your character faces it—*all is lost*? If you can get out of it, all is not lost.

If _____, _____, and then _____ happens, all is lost.

Find what "all is lost" means to your hero. No shortcuts, no pulled punches. This moment is essential.

Structure

Structure has plenty of names, theories, and ridiculous diagrams. Here are a couple of my favorites.

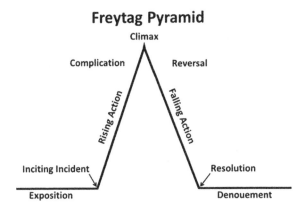

Yup, the first one both induces and alludes to *Vertigo*. The second one looks all nice and pretty, and makes the second half of your story intentionally boring. Let's take a different route.

There are structuralists, anti-structuralists, and structural gurus. There's plenty to say about it, though almost all of it has been said—and said way too often. We'll stick to what matters.

A popular song has verses and choruses. Rarely does the listener pay any attention to either, but the pattern is set in our non-conscious expectations. If a song doesn't present those elements in the accepted manner, our sense of contentedness is shaken. We know something is wrong—but not quite what.

I invited some friends over for dinner one night and had some classic Dave Brubeck playing in the background. My friend Erica was just plain irritable, not her usual state.

Finally, she complained about the music, which had set her on edge. "Take Five" was playing, and Erica wasn't used to hearing music in 5/4 time. The unexpected meter in the music made her pay attention to the dissonance instead of the dinner conversation. The break in her pattern expectation took her focus and annoyed her.

Story structure is the same. When story is experienced in the expected pattern, we pay attention to the story and not its structure. When it breaks that shape or melody, we suddenly focus on the dissonance instead of the story itself. What element is dissonant? When we come out of the story and focus on the structural anomaly, it breaks the effectiveness of the storytelling. We adhere to structure because our audience wants it and we want them. Our brains are wired to be receptive to that pattern.

A story has a beginning, middle, and end. That is the container of the audience member's expectations for the order of a story.

One way of presenting structure is:

Act I—Once upon a time, there was a character who lived in a place . . .

Act II—Then one day, something happens . . . and eventually . . .

Act III—The situation is resolved.

Another version is this:

- Once upon a time . . .

- And then one day . . .

- And just when everything was going so well . . .

- When just at the last minute . . .

- And they all lived happily ever after.

Movies adhere fairly strictly to three-act structure. In Act One, we meet our main character and the world in which she lives. We identify the theme and major elements and have everything we need to send our hero on her journey. Then something big happens to throw the protagonist into Act Two.

Act Two spins the character into action, generally with some upward movement until things fall apart into a complete crisis, a pseudo death. In Act Two, the protagonist makes plans for reaching the goal and is progressively challenged until all is lost.

In Act Three, from the ashes of all is lost, the hero faces the ultimate confrontation and resolves it. She is changed by the experience.

Act One is usually one quarter of your total number of pages, words, or scenes, whichever applies. Act Two is half the story, often with a dramatic moment at the midpoint, smack in the middle at the 50% mark. Act Three is, again, a quarter of the length.

Each act has a job. Act One introduces us to the milieu of the story and to our hero, who, regardless of age or experience, is an innocent as to the material in this particular story. For example, in *As Good As It Gets*, Jack Nicholson is an older, world-weary man of a certain age, but he is childlike in his knowledge of mature relationships and meaningful communication. He is an innocent at the art of life. He's about to be challenged and learn a whole lot, and we get to learn along with him.

Something happens at the end of Act One that throws our story into high speed, and our character must react and plan the journey.

Act Two is the meat of the story. Our hero has plans, but is challenged. The plot becomes more complicated, often with subplots, and eventually the situation gets the better of our hero, until there is a moment when the character and the audience feel that all is lost. In *E.T.*, a movie with perfect structure, E.T. is dead on the operating table. It is the moment in the story when all is lost. In *Black Panther*, King T'Challa lies dead and Killmonger has taken the throne.

Act Three is a form of return, when everything our hero has learned comes into play. Tactics and weapons become skills and wisdom, and the ultimate threat is overcome. The Hero's Journey is complete, and the hero can rejoin her world as a sage figure with wisdom to share in her community. We the audience have shared the journey and gained the wisdom of it. You the writer are wiser.

Scene Order

Scenes proceed in an order of *cause and effect.* Once again, this looks easy but is hard.

Cause and effect means that the events in the preceding scene (scene A) must trigger the events in scene B. The events in A *require* that we go to scene B *next*. Scene A doesn't just precede scene B, but propels us into scene B necessarily.

Cause and effect is how we humans make sense of the world. Cause and effect means that A causes B causes C causes D, ever onward. Without it, it could be A-D-B-A or D-B-Q-X. The world could be entirely arbitrary, with nothing connected to anything else except by chance. Life would be random and complicated. Cause and effect allows us to believe (however falsely) that events are related and that we have some control over them. It allows us to predict what comes next and prepare for it. It allows us to feel a sense of efficacy in our own lives.

This consideration of the signal importance of cause and effect prepares the ground for understanding its importance to your story. If events just happen, your readers will put down your writing. They will hate the sense of randomness and so will you, the writer. It may present a lot of pretty words and impulses, but it isn't a story and, for us, it has no utility. That's how important cause and effect is.

When we write a story, we are required to present the events in a cause-and-effect order. This sequence helps all of us make sense of our world, and, importantly, allows the reader to confidently surrender to the story.

We order the scenes in a sequence which we believe will best keep the reader's interest. How do we do that? Each scene requires the protagonist to go to the next scene in order to achieve her goal. As David Mamet explains, "Dramatic structure consists of the creation and deferment of hope. That's basically all it is. The reversals, the surprises, and the ultimate conclusion of the hero's quest please [the audience] in direct proportion to the plausibility of the opponent forces."[17]

We lay down the order of our scenes and thus the story as if they are train tracks because story is indeed a freight train going at full speed without ever jumping the guard rails. Include every scene required to move your story forward. If a scene isn't necessary, its only function will be to divert the reader's attention. The train will jump the tracks.

Remember that gnawing feeling that having an uncomplicated goal was too simplistic? Sequencing is the moment that the "uncomplicated" goal becomes elegant. By this point, the writers who insisted on nuanced goals are weeping. Their story is too long and too prolix, and they've no idea what to cut.

If you have a solid, simple goal, you can look at every scene in your main plot and ask whether it is directly related to your protagonist achieving the, yes, simple goal you set out at the beginning. If the scene doesn't move the protagonist toward that simple goal, cut the scene. Period.

Look at each scene and ask whether the story could continue on its tracks without that one scene. If the answer is yes, then cut the scene. Cut it mercilessly. If you aren't exactly sure what the scene adds to the story, cut the scene. If it doesn't either tell us something important about the character or move the action forward in a required manner, cut the scene. Your reader won't want to follow you off the tracks and into the scenery—pun intended. Our readers gift us with specific concentration and focus. Don't throw away that gift with complications and layers of fog.

Tentpoles

How do we structure our stories? How do we shape them? We determine what the important events in the story are. We put them in the best order we can come up with, and we call them *tentpoles*. They are the scenes that will support the rest of the structure.

What are the important events or scenes in your story?

To build a story, you need a list of the elements to be included.

These are the moments in the beginning of the story:

- How do we meet the protagonist?

- The antagonist?

- What does the world of the protagonist look like at the beginning?

- Who are the important characters in your hero's world?

- What matters to the hero?

- What does the hero want?

These are the moments in the middle of your story:

- What is your protagonist's plan to achieve the goal?

- What event hurls her forward into action?

- Who are the friends, helpers, mentors, and other characters she needs along the way?

- What goes wrong?

- What else goes wrong?

- What else goes wrong?

- What is the "all" in all is lost?

These are the moments of the resolution of your story:

- What does your hero do when faced with the ultimate challenge?

- What strength, change, or piece of wisdom does the hero use to face the challenge?

- Who wins the challenge . . . and how?

- What does your hero do with the new wisdom in order to bring it back to her ordinary world?

This isn't a checklist. Only you know what events you need to tell your story. Answering those questions will help you see your material and identify the most important moments in your story.

Make a list of the moments in your story. What looks like a good Act I break? Is there a scene that throws the hero into the main action of the story? That's the end of Act I. If not, why not?

Try to find these specific scenes and use them as eleven tentpoles:

Act I:

- the opening

- a real complication

- a turn into the action

Act II:

- a scene that sets out the proposed journey's plan

- a moment when things are going right, and we are hopeful

- a scene where things turn decidedly bad for the hero

- the moment when all is lost

Act III:

- the moment of recommitting to achieve the goal or moment of learning

- the ultimate conflict with the antagonist

- resolution (victory!)

- return to the ordinary world with the wisdom gained by the journey

Those are the 11 scenes that are pivotal to any story. When we feel we have the correct 11 scenes on which the whole story will hang, we'll have our tentpoles. We will have defined the structure and rhythm of the story.

It's time to fill out the story with a *beat sheet*.

A what?

The Beat Sheet

Let's figure out everything that happens in your story and make a list of the events. Yes, you are ready. Yes, it's a lot. And, yes, you are the only one who can figure out what your story needs.

It's time to shape the story.

Novelists write outlines. Everyone writes bullet points. And PowerPoints. Screenwriters write beat sheets. A beat sheet is a list of all the beats in your story. A *beat* is a necessary thing that happens in your story. It can be emotional (a character realizes her lover has been cheating) or a specific incident (the car crashes into the tree). Realizations and emotional moments can be very important to the development of the story, and if they require a major character to behave in a changed manner, they are beats. Most beats are incidents, which require the character to change behavior, impelling the story forward.

A beat is something that must change the course of the story or your principal character. If it doesn't change things, it's not a beat. It's fluff. If you can take it out of the story and the story doesn't change, it's not a beat and it needs to be cut. Conversely, if deleting the beat makes the story fall apart, like pulling at a thread and the whole sweater goes with it, then it's a beat.

The beat sheet for the first pages of *The Godfather* might start like this:

1. Meet the Godfather. How he does business with a supplicant.

2. Connie's wedding. Meet the family.

3. FBI watching. It's the mob.

4. Godfather and Tom dole out favors.

5. Meet Luca Brasi. Meet Michael and Kay.

6. Meet Johnny Fontaine, singing heartthrob.

7. Michael tells Kay the story of helping Johnny. Luca Brasi holds a gun to someone's head. Makes an offer he can't refuse.

The beat sheet is for your own use, so don't put in explanations or descriptions. You know who each of the characters is, so you don't have to put down anything general about them. You do need to say "meet the family" because bringing in your cast of characters is essential and if you cut the scene, we wouldn't know who the characters are or how they are related to each other. The FBI presence tells us we are on the wrong side of the law. We need to see Luca Brasi to understand that he's an assassin and that he's afraid of the Godfather. Johnny Fontaine will be an important character, so meeting him also matters. And right there at page 11, we are introduced to the Godfather's methods of enforcement and the classic line that sets the tone for the rest of the movie: "My father made him an offer he couldn't refuse." Every one of these beats is essential to the story. There is nothing extra.

Here's another example, the opening ten pages of *Spotlight*:

1. At a police station. An abusive priest.

2. Bishop schmoozes victim's mother.

3. Bishop shepherds priest away. Police do nothing.

4. At *Boston Globe.* Meet Robby.

5. Meet other members of the Spotlight team.

6. New editor about to be installed.

7. Robby and Marty, the new editor. Will there be staff cuts?

8. Marty's first editors meeting. Marty asks about an old article about an abusive priest. Robby hears the order to investigate.

Again, the first ten pages, like the opening in any story you or I would write, has to introduce us to our hero's ordinary world and the characters we will need in our story. But, at around page ten in a screenplay, you'll throw some gas on the fire.

A beat sheet is a list of your proposed story points in the proposed order. "Proposed" appears twice in that sentence to underscore that nothing, yet, is written in stone. The sheer number of beats, the order, the significance—they are all up for grabs at this stage.

I prefer beat sheets to outlines because an outline feels more rigid and, much more importantly, allows for sentences or even whole paragraphs of explanation. It allows for fudging on focus. A true beat only takes a few words to communicate. "Darth is Luke's father." E.T. says "phone home." Using a beat sheet is an exercise in focusing each scene in your story on its most important element. If it takes you a paragraph to describe, you probably don't know what that single moment is.

I'm not quite sure why novelists write outlines. It could be to practice some of the language, or to get a feel for each scene, or to get an agent. Some novelists I've worked with go on and on in their outlines, describing the weather, the clothing, the song coming from the speakers. All of that is surplus.

The elements of the story are all we want to know on a beat sheet. It's for your own use only. It's how you organize your story without character, scenery, or diversions.

If you are working on a beat sheet, excess means failure. If what happens in that beat doesn't propel the story to the next scene, then the one you are writing can be cut, and must be cut, because it is somehow a diversion from the fast-moving freight train that is your story.

The beat sheet, in the end, is the train track. Every place that your story must go is on it. Everything else is cut.

Why is the beat sheet so important? Because if it's on there, it's essential. If it's not essential, it's off. Perfect. It not only tells you what to include, it gives you the perfect device to decide what you will have to cut later when, inevitably, you are lost in your own story.

There is no smelling of roses in a well-written story. No slowing down of the freight train. When the writer slows down, the audience falls asleep or leaves. When you and I as writers slow down in the story process, we're diverting our own attention, probably because the very next real beat is too challenging to face today.

Don't get diverted.

If your pantser instincts are kicking in and you just *have to* go write, then go write. But come back for the *Laying of the Cards.*

The Laying of the Cards

In some ritual healing traditions, the healer lays hands on the sufferer and, miraculously, in the moment that the hands are upon the body, the subject is alchemically transformed into someone better and happier. The laying out of the cards for your story can have the same impact. Let's try.

Get a pack of index cards and put each important beat from your beat sheet onto a card. You can leave out the scenes that are transitional or character-based. Lay out the important story points on the cards on a big table, in order.

Now, the big question: Are the scenes laid out in the best possible order?

If you reverse the sequence of a few scenes, can you heighten the drama?

Looking at the *Spotlight* beat sheet, we have the following scenes in this order:

- Meet the protagonist.

- Meet Robby's team.

- Find out there is going to be a new editor.

- Meet the new editor. Possible staff cuts.

- Marty, the new editor, holds his first editorial meeting. Soft assignment of priest story to Robby's team.

Spotlight is a well-made finished product, so it's hard to imagine the scenes in any other order. But what if we put the #4 scene, where we meet the new editor and find out there could be staff cuts and Robby would have to cut some people, before the #2 scene, where we meet Robby's team:

- Meet the protagonist.

- Marty's first editors meeting. Soft assignment of priest story to Robby's team.

- Meet the new editor. Will there be staff cuts?

- Meet the other members of the Spotlight team.

If we see that Robby is worried that there will be staff cuts, then when we meet the other members of the team, we the audience will be wondering who is going to get the ax and how Robby might make that decision. Robby's relationship with his team will be much more tense. There are stories in which that would be a good change, but is it a good change in *this* story?

What if we move the cards around so they look like this:

- Robby gets the soft assignment to look into the abuse cases.

- Robby and new editor Marty have their first meeting, over lunch. Will there be staff cuts?

- Then we meet the team.

In this order, Marty's interest in the priest story will seem much more like a direct order from Robby's new boss. Robby is likely going to follow the order, no matter what. What's his attitude about that? Is he already pissed at the new editor, even before we meet his team? And the staff cuts? Well, even Robby is going to look at his team and wonder how to handle the assignment. Are any of them Catholic? Is that going to be a problem? Doesn't the team usually choose its own assignments, so getting ordered to do the priest abuse story might really annoy the reporters? Are the staff writers resentful? Is there tension now between the staff writers and the new editor?

In the film itself, we meet Robby and then his team members. Because we see them before the idea of cutting staff is presented, we see Spotlight as the team whose members are Robby and the writers. We give up some tension between Robby and his team members but gain more tension between the team as a whole and the editor. Which tensions are better for the story? Do we want to see tension between Robby and the journalists, or do we want to see tension between all the writers as a unit versus the editor or the priests?

Later in *Spotlight*, major scenes are presented in the following order:

- The publisher tells Marty (the editor) to pursue a court order against the church.

- Montage of team doing research. Find out there is another abuser priest.

- Ben (another editor) threatens to kill the story.

- Team members dig in to push back against threat to story.

- Marty meets with the Cardinal. They are adversaries.

- Interview with victims. Learn much more about the abuse, sympathetic victims.

What would happen if we saw Marty and the Cardinal and the lines being drawn between them *before* the publisher authorizes the editor to pursue the court order? There would be a *lot* more drama in deciding to pursue the court order, because it would be a more frontal attack on the Church. More drama is good. But it might send us off into a legal drama instead of a personal drama and thus change the essential nature of the piece.

Every decision accumulates in shaping your story. Where could we put the victim interviews? There's real emotion in the victim scenes. If they go before the publisher scene and the Cardinal scene, we will hate the Cardinal when we meet him. If we already know, through the victims, that the Cardinal is evil, have we changed the tone of the entire story? Will it be about getting the Cardinal? Will it draw attention away from the efforts of the Spotlight team? The victims? Which line of sympathy is the most important? The victims offer the greatest amount of pure emotional connection, but do you and I, as the rewriting authors of *Spotlight*, want the emotional through line to be about the victims, which would be juicy, or about the reporters, who are less emotionally juicy but more heroic?

There are no right and no wrong answers to these questions. The point is that you and I as the writers have the power to order the scenes in the progression we believe will have the most impact *for whatever we choose to be the most important values in our story*. The sequence of our scenes is important.

New writers approach a story as if the vision they have in their head at the beginning of the writing is the only order in which it can be told. But as new *authors* we have *authority* over the story, and the elements are ours to arrange and rearrange as we search for the greatest impact.

There is no single correct way to tell a story. Lay out the cards. Then lay them out differently. And differently again. See if you can improve the drama in your story.

You embrace the power you have over your story when you play with sequencing. If changing the order of scenes makes the hero's road even more intense and difficult, then make the change. If it deepens the conflict, then it's a good change. Remember, we left the transition scenes out of the card pile, because when we reorder scenes, we will have to get from one scene to another in a new way. Don't worry about the transitions now. Just get the events in your story into the sequence that maximizes the tension for your characters.

Can you make your story more compelling?

Raising the stakes is a well-worn cliché that writing instructors use the world over. If you've heard it, you've probably been tempted to put a murder in your mystery, making it seem, you think, scarier. And if that hasn't made the road hard enough for your protagonist, you were told to raise the stakes again, so you put in a kidnapping plot. On the third verse of raising the stakes, you put in some guns and bullets. If you followed this advice, you changed your mystery into a thriller, without conforming the underlying structure. The stakes will be bigger but less effective. You will have pulled your readers out of one genre and into another one, and they'll focus on what's dissonant instead of what matters in the story. You've messed up a good thing.

Raising the stakes doesn't mean you should put bigger, more action-packed beats into the story. It means you should make the elements you already have in the piece more deeply emotional and affecting. Raising the stakes doesn't mean go big. It means *go deep*.

How do you go deep? This is the moment to remember the psychology of your main character. We non-consciously identify with the main character, so we care about the difficulties she suffers in her journey. To that end, the main character must be deeply emotionally affected by the order of your story. The story must present *obstacles to your main character's emotional wounds*.

Is a given obstacle a reminder of something terrible that happened in her past? Does it present exactly the problem she most feared at the beginning of the story? Has she failed to overcome similar obstacles and been shamed about her failure by someone she loves?

These dilemmas deepen the obstacles for your hero and increase our identification with her. If she isn't hurt enough at the end of the second act, go back and, again, be the sadist. We raise the stakes by making the situation more psychologically affecting. It's all about the emotion. Not the car crashes.

Have you reordered your cards so you maximize the drama inherent in each scene? Great!

You need to get the transitions from one event to another back into some order. Figure out what new transitions will get your character to proceed in the most dramatic order and still make sense.

Have you finished the laying of the cards?

If you're a plotter, you probably have a pretty detailed outline now. If you must, go off and write. But come back for the *reduction sauce.*

The Reduction Sauce

Take out a single index card and your favorite writing instrument. Yes, this must be done by hand, slowly, in your most careful writing. It must be done with clarity of mind and purpose.

On one side of the index card, in handwriting no smaller than you can read without your glasses, write down, in order, your list of essential beats in your story, no more than eleven of them.

Read it back to yourself until you are sure these are the most important ones you have.

Now take the other cards, beat sheets, and working papers and affectionately place them in a drawer for a while.

Take the one index card, which is your road map to your story, and place it somewhere convenient. It is your reminder of the essential moments of your story, and it is now all you need.

If you have your tentpoles, you have your act structure. Everything else may change in your story, but if your structure is right and your act breaks are solid, the structure won't change. The foundation of your house has been built. The concrete has dried.

You are almost ready to write. Remember that your job is to write to the end of the piece. It only has a forward gear. No fixing, no editing, no going backward, no doubting. There's plenty of time to fix everything endlessly in all your later drafts. For your first draft, your inner editor and inner critic are banned from the space in your head. Don't let them in. If they slip by, identify them, ruthlessly toss them aside, and stomp on them.

You are ready for the sweetest words in writing.

Go write.

Writing

Build yourself your best environment, put on your special outfit, place the Do Not Disturb sign on the door, pour cups of your favorite beverage, prepare an infinite supply of sharp yellow pencils, fire up the printer, put on your favorite music, dance yourself into a frenzy, become your fullest pantser, and *go write*. Write with abandon. Write with frenzy. Write all id, no superego. Lose yourself. Go write.

Come back when you're finished with your first pass.

The Rewrite

When you write a story, you're telling yourself the story. When you rewrite, your main job is taking out all the things that are NOT the story.

—STEPHEN KING[18]

You've worked your ass off, you put everything you've got into it, and you have yourself a story.

Most writers need a huge serving of praise at this point. Feel free to indulge by emailing a draft to one or two of your best friends, or your partner, mother, sister, or any other entirely reliable other. Tell them their job is to praise you. And by all means, inhale all the praise.

Then get over it and get back to work.

The job of the rewrite isn't to gain praise. The job of the rewrite is to make your piece better. Select a few different readers whom you trust for their ruthless honesty. Their job is to tell you what doesn't work. Listen carefully to their comments. Take in every one of them.

If you are fortunate enough to have more than one good reader, pay special attention to the bumps and comments that more than one person offers about a particular aspect of your story. If a few readers are uncomfortable in the same place in your story, you have a bump you must fix.

The key to taking comments is well explained by Neil Gaiman, who said, "Remember: when people tell you something's wrong or doesn't work for them, they are almost always right. When they tell you exactly what they think is wrong and how to fix it, they are almost always wrong."[19]

My personal experience is that Gaiman's comment is entirely accurate. Your readers know when you fudged or flew over a problem or otherwise dropped the ball. And because we are writing for readers both real and imaginary, their opinions of where we failed them or lost the story are incredibly valuable. They identify the bumps in the story. Your job is to address the bumps and even it out. You can try to argue them out of it, but it's already too late. The readers are the jury, and when the render a verdict of "bump," it's binding.

Their suggestions for how to fix the problem will always be wrong. Only you know your character well enough to go deeper to find the answer. Only you understand how to address your character's wound. You are the god of the kingdom you have created, and sometimes being all-powerful is a hard gig.

What's the most predictable problem in your first draft? Almost always, it's what happens at the bottom of the second act. What happened when all was lost? The problems come in two flavors:

1. All is not lost: You took it easy on your character.

2. All is very lost, and you can't get them out of the hell you built.

All Is Not Lost

If the bottom of your Act II took it easy on your hero, don't worry. You can almost always make it worse. Were you truly brutal? Is the situation irredeemable? Did you throw all the worst of the worst at her?

How bad does it have to get at the bottom of the second act? It's usually a sort of death, including the sort where someone in fact dies. In *Black Panther*, T'Challa has been heaved over a waterfall and fallen to his death. In *E.T.*, E.T. is so dead that he's been pronounced dead by all the scientists. In *Field of Dreams*, the dream is dead.

Does your character suffer the actual death of a loved one? Of a goal? Of a dream? Does your character suffer a pseudo death—the death of the soul or spirit? Your hero doesn't have to be physically dead, but in the sense of the journey that you have made her travel, she must suffer at least a pseudo death or a death of all hope.

Yes, there's a fill in for this:

My hero suffered the death of _____.

She suffered the death of her body, spirit, love, hope, future.

Go back and be even more sadistic. Enjoy it. How often do you have permission to be your most evil self?

Seriously, go be your baddest. But do come back.

All Is Too Lost

Ah, this is great. You dug your hero into such a deep hole that you can't get her out of it.

This feels like hell for the writer. My carpets are worn out in the circle in front of my desk from my walking, running, stomping, damn near digging while I searched for ways for my heroes to lift themselves out of the horrible holes I had thrown them in. Here's the good news: You will find a way out, and it will transform your story.

At the bottom of the second act, your character—and that bit of your sub-conscious that was there for the creation of that very hole—has run out of known fixes, moves and rationalizations to get herself out of the hole. Your conscious and your sub-conscious have no answers. And this is great! We've crystallized a problem you've probably carried around with you, in real or fictional form, for a long time. And you have no old answers.

This is the golden moment. You must create something new, something you have never thought of before, but which is well within your capacities and knowledge. You just haven't put it together yet.

Creativity is the act of making something entirely new out of two already known materials. It is that spark, that step into the unknown. It's time to be creative in the deepest sense of the word.

Use whatever techniques worked for you in opening the

door to your story. Go meditate, dream, garden, sew, dance. Turn your brain over to daydreaming. Allow your non-conscious mind to cook on it. Yes, it can take days. If you think the act of creation is quick, you are in the wrong business. It's hard, it takes a bit of time . . . and it is brilliant.

If you can't get the hero out of the hole, try some of these techniques:

- Write the end of Act II from the perspective of the other characters who are present. When you change your perspective, you get new information to include.

- Go back to your statement of the goal your character had set. Now make that goal more spiritual or internal. What has your character learned about herself that now must become material? Can the doctor who wanted merely to live a cushy life realize that a good doctor has to do good for the patients? Did the lawyer learn that she didn't merely want to practice law but also that she had to champion justice and truth? What are the deeper meanings of the original goal?

- What has your hero discovered along the way?

You have just put your hero through hell for the whole second act. Simply put, what has she learned?

In the absolute worst-case scenario, it is possible that the thing your character has learned is that there is, in fact, no way out. Sound ridiculous? Take a look at the classic romance, *An Officer and a Gentleman*. The hero's goal was to make it as an aviator in the US Navy. He was scrubbing out. The script had exactly this problem: a hole the writers couldn't get the hero out of. Producers, studio executives, directors, writers, people on the street all came to the same conclusion: There's no way to get the Richard Gere character out of the hole.

Finally, the team gave up. They gave Gere a single line: "I got nowhere else to go!" In effect, Gere surrenders to failure. He throws in the towel. He suffers a spiritual or pseudo death. He is a complete failure. He has no choice but to go forward and grow. Amazingly, it works. We believe that he finds previously unknown strengths, values his romantic relationship, and honors his military seniors, because he has, in effect, made his goal even deeper: not just to be in the service, but to be the manifestation of the values that being in the service means.

If your character is still in the hole, ask yourself what greater understanding can she find? What deeper meaning is available? What truth hasn't yet been addressed? What is *more true*? Your hero must now make the leap from an ordinary character to a special person, a wiser one.

Allow your brilliant mind to show you where and how to make the great leap.

Remember, this is the richest moment in your writing. Almost everything you have done thus far has led you to this magnificent, unsettling point. Your victory, like that of your protagonist, comes in this moment of rising through the difficulties presented with greater understanding, depth, and wisdom.

The goal of the rewrite is to make that moment of near death into the beginning of the sequence of rebirth. How does your character change? What is the lesson that makes everything different? What is the wisdom gained?

Once you develop the sequence from near death to bigger life, go rewrite as much as you want. Let your inner editor go nuts. Invite your inner critic to the party. Be as persnickety as you can be.

My hero learned that even though she thought _____.

The deeper meaning of her goal is that _____.
Do you have that transformational moment? If so, great. Go rewrite.

And in the End . . .

Embrace the journey. Smooth out all the bumps. Revel in the victory over the antagonist in Act III. And remember: The duty of the hero is to bring the wisdom of the journey back to her community. Bring the boon to the world. In *Black Panther*, T'Challa opens up a youth center at the very location of the original sin, the abandonment of Killmonger. He ends the isolation of the Wakandans, not with armaments but with acts of deep kindness toward the outside world.

The Lemonade

Why Writing Stories Changes Your Life

What happens when we read an engaging story? First we tend to lose our self-consciousness as we float into the world of the story. If we are further absorbed by the story, our sense of the real world around us disappears. "If we are so involved with the story that our real world disappears and we project ourselves more fully into a story, psychologists say we are *transported*. We conceptualized transportation into a narrative world as a distinct mental process, an integrative melding of attention, imagery, and feelings."[20]

"Transportation is defined as 'a convergent process, where all mental systems and capacities become focused on events occurring in the narrative.'"[21] "People lose track of time and fail to observe events going on around them; a loss of self-awareness may take place."[22] "The narrative world is distant from the world in which the reader lives and makes it possible that the events in the story are perceived as real within the story context, even when events would not be possible in reality."[23]

The most intense interaction of the reader and the protagonist that I have found in the literature is this transportation of the reader into the fictive world. At that level of involvement, the impact of the fiction is heightened yet again. Entering this imaginary world, we throw off even more of the restraints of the real world. We are even less likely to have concern for factual accuracy or critical analysis. We become oblivious to false notes. When we as audience members are transported into a story, we are ever more likely to experience the events as truly personal, and we are thereby more apt to be changed by what happens on the page to a fictional character.

We feel what the character feels. We learn what the character learns. In the real world, we reality-check all the time, running a doubt filter to make sure we don't get fooled. We turn it way down when we read. Because we accept the world as the story presents it, *we internalize the experience without doubt.*

We know that reading a book can change someone's life. By reading about someone else's journey, we have simulated that experience, and gained the benefits and wisdoms of that journey. If the protagonist comes out not just wiser but happier, then we, too, have absorbed the lessons of the journey and the happiness as well. Keep reading, and your little happiness bonus units will keep adding up.

Our absorption in story not only changes how we feel in that moment, but also *changes our behavior.*[24] The more involved we are with the fiction, the greater is our ability to change ourselves. We have made this progress simply by being couch potatoes and passively observing that journey by reading. If each level of involvement increases the power of the vicarious experience of the journey of the protagonist while you are passively reading, can you imagine the huge jump in impact when you go from passively viewing it to actively creating it?

Reading can light a lovely flame of change for us. If we want more than that, we have to use the magic fire accelerant. Let's light it up. What's the accelerant? Well, writing, of course.

What happens when we write a story? Imagine writing the scene in *Jaws* when the previously unseen shark attacks the swimming boy. We can imagine the writer seeing all of the action from an objective perspective. We writers would need to go into the minds of our characters. The writer will start by going into the boy's mind. We experience the boy kicking away, maybe he gets a little seawater in his mouth, spits it out, looks up at the seashore to wave to mom and dad, and continues swimming. That's the first perspective.

We would also go into the mind of the shark. We only have a shark brain, so all we think is "umm, hungry, umm, food." We close in on the prey and take a good bite. "Umm, good." The shark feels some satisfaction. That is the second perspective.

But we are in the shark's mind and we can see the results of our shark-action. We can observe the terror on the kid's face and the gruesome sight of the child's limb torn from the body, the blood in the water. We hear screams as the effects of the attack play out. Do we still feel "umm, hungry, umm, good"? Do we *also* have some empathy for the kid and some horror at the damage we have just caused?

We have experienced both being victimized by a man-eating shark and also victimizing the young boy. Haven't we, as the shark, just changed how we see our self because we feel empathy for the victim? If we "go inside" two characters in the same interaction, the experience is additive, and your empathic response changes you.

The writer has just experienced two levels of theory of mind, the shark and the kid. What if we add a third level of awareness?

This very question is dramatized in the movie *Disney's The Kid*. Bruce Willis plays Russ Duritz, an image consultant. Russ's childhood self, Rusty, played by Spencer Breslin, comes to visit Russ. Where Russ is smooth, Rusty is a dork. The story asks, what can Rusty do to be less dorky? Or the reverse, what can Russ do to be more accepting of his flawed self? What event caused this transformation from dorky to cool? And is it a good thing? Russ is, after all, not just attractive but insensitive and repressed as well.

In the film, young Rusty gets to relive a traumatic event from his past while Russ looks on. Rusty has done something wrong, and his father reprimands him. Rusty starts to cry. Dad then yells at him. When Rusty tries to control his tears, he develops a twitch. We writers are in Rusty's mind and he is overwhelmed and frightened.

Now we have to go into Dad's mind. What's going on there? Dad is angry and tells Rusty that his mom is sick and "we could lose her." Does Rusty understand this? No, he's still a child with a narcissistic mindset, wondering how to not get yelled at.

Can Dad understand what this is doing to Rusty? No, he's overwhelmed by his fear of losing his wife. We have no synthesis of the points of view.

What do we do now? We writers need to create another perspective on this event. How about having Russ watch this interaction? Russ can watch and try to understand the experience from within the minds of both Rusty and Dad. Russ represents the next (third) level of consciousness. He can feel how frightened the kid is. He can feel how angry the dad is. He can also feel, as the kid cannot, how terrified the father is about the potential loss of his wife. This is information not available to the kid and not quite cognizable in the dad.

Russ thus provides an additional, more elevated and empathetic awareness or theory of mind. He can imagine the separate consciousness of the kid, who is frightened because Dad is yelling at him. He is also into Dad's mind while the man is shouting because the father is terrified, overwhelmed, and weak. From Russ's point of view, the dad, who has only been a tough disciplinarian in the past, is now *also* vulnerable and flawed. He isn't frightening to Russ anymore, but rather more nuanced and worthy of compassion.

This understanding transforms the relationship between Russ and Dad. Russ knows the father never intended to hurt his son; the father was just having a fully human moment of freaking out in front of his son because the man's wife is dying. And Rusty was scarred by the event because he couldn't experience his father's fear. We can understand the emotions of each of the two characters, but they are still at loggerheads. The two perspectives understand, but are too limited to resolve the situation. For that beneficial outcome, we need a third point of view. We need Russ. He gives us the compassionate outlook that synthesizes the event into an adult, empathetic perspective. Whew.

Russ's consciousness is different from, and wiser than, either of the previous levels of theory of mind. Adding Russ's POV makes the entire experience that much more intense, memorable, and transformative. That's the importance of the additional layer. It brings us more nuance, more depth, more opportunity to grow.

But who is watching this scene or reading this story? We writers must necessarily consider, and enter, yet another level of consciousness. Our job is to entertain and engage the audience. What's going on inside the folks sitting on the couch, watching the movie or reading the book about the three fictional characters? How the audience is processing the story is crucial to our job as writers. How are the actions of Rusty (1) and the reactions of Dad (2) integrated by Russ (3) and processed in the minds of the audience (4)? What benefit is that to us, this fourth level of theory of mind? By watching Russ integrate the information, we the audience learn how to integrate information, and that has an impact on our ability to grow and change. Each additional level of consciousness brings with it additional benefits, if we can keep it all straight. We go into the mind of the reader or audience member because our job is to effectively communicate the story. When we review our writing and ask whether "it works," we are asking what is going on in the mind of our audience member. If it doesn't work, we have failed and have to try again. If it works, we've brought the message home to its target, that additional layer of mind.

But wait, can we add yet another beneficial level of understanding? Of course! Someone had to think up Rusty, the conflict with Dad, the observations of Russ, and the emotions of the audience! That's right, there's a fifth level of theory of mind, who keeps all this emotional analysis and learning going. It's us! It's the writers! The mind of the writer has to not just passively watch all this, but also must originate it. The writer's mind is always yet another level of consciousness. To adequately do our job, we are challenged to bring yet a further level of understanding, compassion, analysis and wisdom. We may be quiet about it, but we bring a lot of consciousness to the table, and *we receive a lot of benefit from it, if we so choose.*

For some number of years, the Writers Guild tried to bring more respect to the lowly screen and television writers by taking out billboards on Sunset Boulevard with a picture and the written dialogue of famous scenes, with the headline "Someone wrote that." It's as if the Hollywood writers corps was standing on a soap box screaming, "Hey we're the smart ones! We thought it all up!" Or, perhaps they could have shouted, "Hey, we're the smart ones! We bring an additional level of theory of mind!" I grant you that it would be a terrible advertising slogan, but it would have the benefit of being true, at least the theory of mind part. When we write, we have the minds of all the characters in the scene before us. We go in and become each of them, with straight empathy and theory of mind.

But writing is different. Writing is *active.* We don't just watch these characters' minds; we choose, direct, and express their feelings and thoughts. We are transformed into all the characters and the synthesized content of the totality of the scene.

When we write, we are in the brain of a character when that character speaks. Then we switch to the brain of another character when that character speaks. We don't write dialogue from the outside. We compose dialogue from inside the mind of each character in the first person. We are the first person who speaks. Then we go into the second person, the listener, to see how it plays. We might have a third character in the scene, like Russ, who is a synthesizer or pure observer. Russ has the third level of consciousness, which the writer shares. But how is the audience feeling about the scene? The writer has to consider how the audience feels about Russ's synthesis of Dad's anger at Rusty.

We writers are the God-figure living in the head of each and all the characters, understanding all of them at the same time, synthesizing it all, and creating all their emotions and behaviors. We are the fifth level of theory of mind. Writing a story or scene like this requires that the writer exercises an extraordinary sensitivity to and understanding of the minds of all of these people simultaneously as they *react* to each other as they are *moving through time*. The process develops a daunting understanding of other people and of ourselves.

What does it mean for the writer to go inside everyone's mind? Like Russ, the writer will feel empathy *for all sides*. The writer *is* each of them. The bad guy isn't all bad. The good guy is flawed. We transform our emotions about the victimizers to have empathy for what drove them in the first place. We don't have to like them for it, but we will have a level of understanding, *and that takes the onus off your character for having the flaws in the first place*. Dad yelling at Rusty? Well, that third level of consciousness could say, Rusty got frightened because he was a kid, and dad was frightened because of mom. . . . Hey, look at that. Dad isn't a monster, he's just human. Rusty isn't a dork, he's just human. Great, we can love them both!

The benefit of the transportation? Do we have to love all our characters, even the child-eating shark? No, we don't. It still ate a child who could not defend himself. But in our horror at the event, we can also see that the shark was following an evolutionary mandate. It wasn't an intentional murder. It was a force of nature, with less malice than we would have expected. We can still hate the antagonist and yet learn from our changed perspective.

As writers and creators, we live in the minds of our characters as they interact with each other, and we learn the lessons they learn. We empathize with everyone. And since characters are pieces of ourselves projected onto the page, we can have more love and empathy for *ourselves*. We can love the pieces of us, not for prideful reasons, but because we have increased our acceptance, empathy, and compassion for others and ourselves.

When we face a crisis by writing stories, we use the circumstances to increase our own empathy and humanity, and thus heal ourselves and enrich our souls. What a lovely way to use a crisis.

Endnotes

1 "Rahm Emanuel on the Opportunities of Crisis," *Wall Street Journal* CEO Council in Washington, D.C., November 19, 2008, https://www.youtube.com/watch?v=_mzcbXi1Tkk.

2 James W. Pennebaker and Sandra K. Beall, "Confronting a Traumatic Event. Toward an Understanding of Inhibition and Disease," *Journal of Abnormal Psychology* 95, no. 3 (August 1986): 274–281, doi:10.1037//0021-843x.95.3.274.

3 Ibid.

4 James W. Pennebaker and John F. Evans, *Expressive Writing: Words that Heal* (Enumclaw, WA: Idyll Arbor, 2014), 3 et seq.

5 Brynne C. DiMenichi et al., "Writing About Past Failures Attenuates Cortisol Responses and Sustained Attention Deficits Following Psychosocial Stress," *Frontiers in Behavioral Neuroscience* 12 (2018), doi:10.3389/fnbeh.2018.00045.

6 James W. Pennebaker and Joshua M. Smyth, *Opening Up by Writing It Down: How Expressive Writing Improves Health and Eases Emotional Pain* (New York: The Guilford Press, 2016), 23.

7 Pennebaker and Evans, *Expressive Writing*, 43 et seq.

8 Ibid., 48.

9 Ibid., x.

10 Sophie Nicholls, "Beyond Expressive Writing: Evolving Models of Developmental Creative Writing," *Journal of Health Psychology* 14, no. 2 (March 2009): 174, doi:10.1177/1359105308100201.

11 Mai Nguyen, Tamara Vanderwal, and Uri Hasson, "Shared Understanding of Narratives Is Correlated with Shared Neural Responses," *NeuroImage* 184, no. 1 (January 2019): 168, doi: 10.1016/j.neuroimage.2018.09.010.

12 Stephen King, *On Writing* (New York: Simon & Schuster, 2002), 25.

13 Linda L. Seger, *Making a Good Script Great* (Hollywood, CA: Samuel French, 1987), 125.

14 Syd Field, *Screenplay: The Foundations of Screenwriting* (New York: Delta Trade Paperbacks, 2005), 246–247.

15 John Gapper, "Lunch with David Mamet," Slate, June 11, 2011, https://slate.com/human-interest/2011/06/lunch-with-david-mamet-the-dramatist-says-he-s-crazy-about-sarah-palin.html.

16 Kurt Vonnegut's 8 rules for writing a short story, https://blog.bookbaby.com/2013/11/kurt-vonneguts-8-rules-for-writing-a-short-story/.

17 David D. Mamet, *Bambi vs. Godzilla: On the Nature, Purpose, and Practice of the Movie Business* (New York: Vintage Books, 2008), 112.

18 King, *On Writing*, 47.

19 Maria Popova, "Neil Gaiman's 8 Rules of Writing," Brain Pickings, https://www.brainpickings.org/2012/09/28/neil-gaiman-8-rules-of-writing/.

20 Melanie C. Green and Timothy C. Brock, "The Role of Transportation in the Persuasiveness of Public Narratives," *Journal of Personality and Social Psychology* 79, no. 5 (December 2000): 701, doi: 10.1037/0022-3514.79.5.701, citing Melanie C. Green and Timothy C. Brock, "In the Mind's Eye: Transportation-Imagery Model of Narrative Persuasion," in *Narrative Impact: Social and*

Cognitive Foundations, ed. Melanie C. Green, Jeffrey J. Strange, and Timothy C. Brock (Hillsdale, NJ: Erlbaum, in press), n.p.

21 P. Matthijs Bal and Martijn Veltkamp, "How Does Fiction Reading Influence Empathy? An Experimental Investigation on the Role of Emotional Transportation," *PLoS ONE* 8, no. 1 (January 2013): 3, doi:10.1371/journal.pone.0055341, citing Green and Brock, "The Role of Transportation in the Persuasiveness of Public Narratives," 701.

22 Bal and Veltkamp, "How Does Fiction Reading Influence Empathy?," 3, citing Rick Busselle and Helena Bilandzic, "Fictionality and Perceived Realism in Experiencing Stories: A Model of Narrative Comprehension and Engagement," *Communication Theory* 18, no. 2 (May 2008): 255–280.

23 Bal and Veltkamp, "How Does Fiction Reading Influence Empathy?," 3, citing Joshua Goodstein and Deena S. Weisberg, "What Belongs in a Fictional World?," *Journal of Cognition and Culture* 9, no. 1–2 (March 2009): 69–78, doi:10.1163/156853709x414647.

24 Paul J. Zak and Stephen Knack, "Trust and Growth," *The Economic Journal* 111, no. 470 (March 2001): 295–321, doi:10.1111/1468-0297.00609.

About the Author

Samantha Shad was a member of the bar in three states and a practicing entertainment attorney in Beverly Hills before she turned her attention to screenwriting. She wrote twenty feature film scripts for the major studios, including *Class Action* (Twentieth Century Fox), as well as feature length and episodic television for each of the major networks, including the movie *Vanished Without A Trace* (NBC-Universal). She has taught advanced writing, media, and the law at UCLA, The American Film Institute and Pierce College. She now teaches advanced writing and leads seminars on how to Write to Happiness.

She is the author of *The Write to Happiness* and *Write Through the Crisis*.

Visit with her at **samanthashad.com**.

Made in the USA
Coppell, TX
16 April 2020

20324424R00079